CRITICAL
NEIGHBOURHOODS

PARK BOOKS

**CRITICAL
NEIGHBOURHOODS**

**THE ARCHITECTURE OF
CONTESTED COMMUNITIES**

**EDITED BY
PAULO MOREIRA**

LA PALOMERA
Caracas, Venezuela

● **T CAMP**
New Delhi, India

● **CHICALA**
Luanda, Angola

WHAT MAKES A NEIGHBOURHOOD
"CRITICAL"?

PREFACE BY
ABDOUMALIQ SIMONE

All neighbourhoods are "critical" in some way. They all provide a platform of residence and operation for "someone", making a contribution to the overall functioning of the urban that may or may not be recognised or valued.

Recent attention has focused on the widespread evisceration or exhumation of neighbourhoods and neighbourhood life, relegating many populations to the hinterlands, which are often structured as sacrificial areas or insular bastions of predation or purported self-sufficiency. What this project on critical neighbourhoods offers is a systematic way of restoring attention to the capacities of particular districts to offer generative, salient knowledge of what it is possible to do with urban life in all its fragility and brokenness.

Often, the production of history in territorial contexts of this kind occludes or at least obscures the ways in which they attempt to do many things at once and the manner in which these efforts are often relegated to the status of heritage at best, or anachronism at worst. "Critical neighbourhoods" must not only manage the pushes and pulls of heterogeneous aspirations and practices, but at times risk their very stability and endurance in an attempt to proclaim their presence, attainments, and ways of doing things in new arenas. Neighbourhoods are never self-contained; they are never governed by some overarching coherence, based on a set of consensually deliberated cultural assumptions and operating procedures. The frictions between strategies for engaging with the broader urban context, the necessary differentiations between styles and accumulation practices, and the often contrary ways in which alliances are forged result in continuous contestation, require constantly updated translations between different orientations and vernaculars, and render any stable representation of what takes place not only impractical but potentially debilitating.

It is for this reason that the authors have sought to engage with a variety of neighbourhoods in Luanda, Caracas, and New Delhi in a manner that involves archival research, the study and making of maps, plans, drawings, and photographs, and institution building as collaborative data gathering at different scales. They effectively mobilise these methods to make historical connections and reveal the slow dismantling, incremental upgrading, or belaboured infrastructural sustention of a range of neighbourhoods. Here, research takes the form of collaborative projects with residents, community associations, and urban institutions over a protracted period of time. This book is a by-product of these collaborations rather than their ultimate objective. It encompasses a diverse set of media and presentation styles that does not always result in a "smooth fabric" or seamless text, for it is full of "interruptions" (expositions, charts, maps, appendices), but this means that parts of it can be disassembled and reformatted for use in a wider range of functions. While the authors draw on postcolonial urban theories to offer a cogent history of their respective cities, the methods and outcomes are an outstanding example of contemporary architectural research. Each city is rooted in a radically different historical context, yet their shared affective landscape allows them to speak easily to one another. This landscape is shaped by a strong sense of self-validation, and urgency mixed with sporadic resignation, a refusal to be traumatised into complacency, and a patient determination to pursue what might be construed as unrealistic objectives, while simultaneously refusing the easy tropes of redemption.

For what is being marginalised, evicted, or made precarious is not merely the lives and materials of these neighbourhoods but their very "criticality". Whether they are hinges mediating flows across different scales or urban districts, whether they viably accommodate the long- and short-term needs of a footloose population, whether they house a wide range of small-scale factories or embody a vast pool of skilled labour, whether their modes of social reproduction offer implicit propositions of what the city could be, these aspects of criticality are under attack in a rapid unravelling or slow, drawn-out violence.

Too often, urban policy distils the needs of an urban majority – that amalgamation of low income, working and lower middle class residents – into affordable housing, efficient urban services, and adequate infrastructure. These policies are based on a perception of everyday existence as a matter of consumption and of political responsibility as a question of basic provisioning to those who are to be supported as individual citizens, who possess a standard set of rights and responsibilities. In this conception, the neighbourhood revolves around the balanced, systemic distribution of clearly delineated functions and amenities aimed at individuating residents, i.e. treating them as individualised entities, or at least those who are assembled into coherent heteronormative households.

Rather than as a site of balanced distribution, enhanced individuation or embodiment of public endowments, the criticality of the neighbourhood lies in its nature as a self-renovating machine using the densities of composition – of bodies, sentiments, histories, resources, ways of doing things, and networks – to continuously generate new capacities, synergies, vernaculars, and associations, restructuring the terms and interactions involving the different "ingredients". While any specific configuration of interconnections may posit a structured trajectory of where neighbourhoods might be headed, they are also sufficiently aware of the volatile, vulnerable context in which they are situated to shift gears, switch up the ways in which specific agendas are adopted, and alter these agendas. This is not a question of resilience or flexibility. It does not concern the characteristics of residents *per se*, but rather the ways in which they engage with and appropriate the operations of the urban itself.

In this regard, in relations underpinned by contiguity, affinity, instigation, command, or serendipity, we know that cities are full of things that connect and touch upon one another, yet never leave a discernible mark. These *inoperable relations* reset the scale of the city by ceaselessly changing the modulations of social life as if they were always already in sync with a pulsating aesthetics that remains successfully "out of sight". In other words, every house or road built, every market transaction proffered, every gathering held, every material used in a project is part of a process of "touch" and interconnection that stretches far beyond its immediate orbit or visible impact. It is the capacity of neighbourhoods to find ways of embodying these virtual webs of relationality that provides both the impetus and the materials for continuous updating, incremental growth, and, sometimes, overexposure or collapse. Of course, the ability to tap into this embedded world of relationality is not without limits. It is constrained by competing types and levels of authority, external impositions relating to infrastructure and regulation, and internal arrangements that seek to mediate and often temper risk-laden initiatives. Yet it may be viewed as a kind of "general intelligence", an ongoing recalibration of the senses to an environment based on the different registers of signals issued by that environment.

What, then, constitutes a method able to apprehend these processes, this melding of human inhabitation with the diverse and sometimes discordant relational forces that make up the surroundings? This is precisely the challenge taken up by the authors here as they navigate a process of reflection, debate, remembrance, and imagination to develop shifting narratives about the histories and presents that constitute their neighbourhoods. It is a method that acknowledges the realities of multiple, competing genealogies, recognising that what transpired to make the neighbourhood the way it is and posit a limited number of future dispositions is not one thing, not one story or line of causation, but a conjunction of fluctuating forces and figures that may have operated in ways that are not exactly consonant with those that make up the prevailing narrative.

Critical neighbourhoods offer their own critiques of urbanisation processes extending far beyond themselves. They twist and turn in response to multiple conundrums and conditions, taking great risks yet discovering unanticipated ways of doing things in the process. Because they resist and refuse to be pinned down to a single or discernible function, what they reveal is also potentially an archive of the larger city, whose discordant policies, imaginations, and articulations they come to bear.

Neighbourhood as critique, as well as an embodiment of critical functions: this is the shared agenda that the authors seek to document and understand in this important book. A challenge that poses new questions and opportunities for an engaged architecture.

CRITICAL
NEIGHBOURHOODS

The Architecture of
Contested Communities

INTRODUCTION BY
PAULO MOREIRA

We are living in a time of dramatic social and spatial segregation. As expulsions from home and land have become a global phenomenon, many multicultural neighbourhoods are at risk of "extinction" or of assuming a purely economic function. Without an understanding of the true nature and urban vitality of contested communities, a segregationist conceptualisation of the city will inevitably prevail.

This publication analyses three neighbourhoods in culturally diverse urban places on three different continents, seeking to reveal the fullness of life in these places. Looking beyond geographic context, the aim is to learn about human habitat and relate spatial issues to broader economic and political questions, with a particular emphasis on the reciprocity between them.

These neighbourhoods may be classified as "critical" because their institutions and cultures struggle to adapt to the urban milieu in some way. One way of exploring this subject is to look beyond the neighbourhoods' concrete built forms and consider their sociological formation and changing population. Each chapter reflects on the heterogeneity of society and its priorities when it comes to occupying space.

In this book, architecture is understood as a multilayered profession that combines technical know-how with social interaction. The methodological approaches used include ethnographic methods, in-depth interviews, spatial surveys, and collaborative design experiments. We seek innovative ways of understanding the processes that cause socially segregated neighbourhoods to form, with the aim of lending nuance to the hegemonic discourse espoused by some architects, urban practitioners, and civil society organisations, who tend to divide the urban population into homogeneous groups and dismiss the virtues of social diversity.

The book is intended to build stronger links between urban fragments that are often perceived as fractured or unrelated. By drawing connections between the multiple casualties of three types of urban divide, our understanding of the ways in which apparently disconnected neighbourhoods can work and connect with their cities in fruitful ways can grow.

Based on our extensive experience on the ground, we present an inclusive approach to practising architecture and thinking the city, which accepts and includes contested communities. Collaboration is a fundamental tool in enabling these dialogues and engagement to take place. Ultimately, grasping the essence and understanding the reciprocities of complex urban situations is the most likely way to achieve credible praxis.

Methodological framework

Tension and conflict are likely to be present in any neighbourhood facing social segregation or imminent destruction, requiring the development of a series of methods in order to explore the topic. There are no magic formulae for addressing the questions and concerns present in neighbourhoods considered "critical", but some of the techniques used in the fields of sociology, anthropology, and geography can be both feasible and effective.

Nevertheless, methods borrowed from the social sciences are a mere supplement to the more complex, hybrid reach of architectural practice. Architectural studies require a distinctive approach, mobilising different methods to highlight temporal and spatial connections or to reveal the gradual assembling, vitality, and slow dismantling of a neighbourhood. Any exploration of the relationship between the neighbourhood and the city must acknowledge the deeply intertwined nature of spatial analysis, political conflict, and cultural identity.

The methodology employed in architectural investigation is itself subject to research and interpretation. Firstly, we seek to orient our research towards context rather than individual subjectivity. Secondly, we view practical knowledge as the primary vehicle for understanding how different methods contribute to the design/research topic. This methodology draws on the notion of hermeneutics developed by Hans-Georg Gadamer.[1] Hermeneutics is the capacity to explain or interpret, or simply the "art of understanding".[2] "Practice" is in itself a form of understanding. In this book, which is concerned with comprehending specific parts of the world or urban fragments where architecture plays a central role, we seek a hermeneutics of practice.

The outcome of this theoretical and philosophical approach is that we find a way of navigating from very primordial, local experiences of a city's spatiality and materiality to more sophisticated, specialised global discourses (from economics, politics, sociology, etc.) without absorbing architecture into a mere "concept". Rather, the reverse is true: we make concepts answerable to architecture. This results in a far lesser degree of certainty than the methods used in the natural sciences. In other words, the methodological approach employed in these architectural experiences is not a "science" in itself, developing instead amid the uncertainties of sociability and human interchange. On this premise, our studies straddle what is conventionally understood as theory and practice. A combination of methods is used to enable continuous learning and action in solidarity with others.

The evolution of the practical methods employed in a project over time plays a key role in shaping its outcome and our primary methodological concern relates to the manner in which different approaches and results communicate with one another. The methodology used in a project is the product of constant negotiation between the neighbourhood and external institutions. Against this backdrop, a "promiscuity" of methods is preferable if we are to capture the diversity and complexity of the phenomena at work. Exploring the hybrid conditions of a "critical neighbourhood" calls for a hybrid, interdisciplinary methodology.

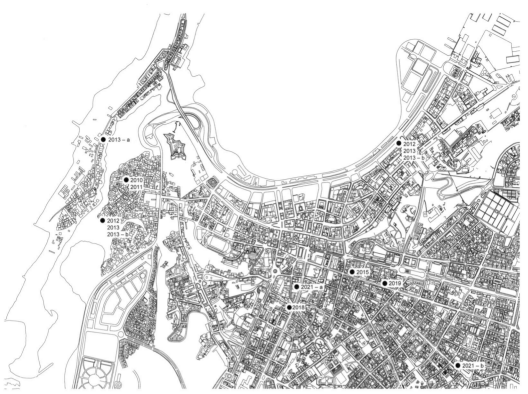

Plan of Luanda showing houses occupied by Paulo Moreira during
fieldwork (2010–2021). © Paulo Moreira, 2021

1 Gadamer's *Reason in
the Age of Science* (1981)
presents three key essays
that are particularly
relevant: "What is Practice?
The Conditions of Social
Reason" (pp. 69–87),
"Hermeneutics as Practical
Philosophy" (pp. 88–112)
and "Hermeneutics as a
Theoretical and Practical
Task" (pp. 113–138).
2 Gadamer, H. G. (1981)
*Reason in the Age of
Science*, p. 113.

Seven methods

A toolkit of seven methods used in architectural projects in contested communities is presented below in no particular order. The connections between the different themes are implicit and overlaps are inevitable.

1.   Primary experience

Getting to know the site is a key part of any design or research project on "critical neighbourhoods". Fieldwork shows us that gaining knowledge is a process of active following, of "going along".[3] Only by living in and experiencing a neighbourhood can we help defend it from external forces with the potential to shatter residents' lives. Gadamer's metaphor echoes this conviction:

> We realise ourselves how hard it is to read aloud a text in a foreign tongue or even a difficult text in one's own language on short notice in such a way that one can make good sense of it. (...) Only when one understands what one is reading can one modulate and introduce a rhythm in such a way that what is meant really comes out.[4]

In some ways, this approach resonates with that of authors such as Charles Booth (who contributed to understanding social problems in nineteenth-century London), Levi Strauss (who observed everyday life in non-Western communities in the mid-twentieth century to identify common human patterns), and Jane Jacobs (who sought to assimilate the language of segregated communities in New York to protect them from total clearance). In different places and epochs, these authors engaged with "critical" urban contexts.

Yet observation and analysis can also become tools of intervention. Sites offer insights and opportunities to demonstrate their spatial and social coherence. By immersing ourselves and our practices in a concrete place, we can witness the urban vitality of a neighbourhood, a city, and their peripheries over a specific period of time.

The scope and objectives of each site visit can vary, while the case study should be identified in collaboration with the site's institutions, encouraging communication and allowing rules to be established (and conflicts to be played out). When undertaking fieldwork in an external context, the issue of passive observation versus active engagement is a recurring dilemma. More often than not, the former is the more common approach among architects and researchers.

We challenge this passive, purely observational stance, advocating for an approach that evolves through personal perceptions and social interactions. This echoes Herbert Gans, who said that by wandering through a given neighbourhood and using it as a local resident, he developed a kind of selective perception, whereby his eyes "focused only on those parts of the area that were actually being used by people".[5]

Engagement with a particular neighbourhood and with the city as a whole, which should be evident in all architectural projects, prompts a constant rethinking of the procedures used in conventional research. The platforms of engagement with people and institutions that result from this process are thus based on an understanding of the specific cultural, political, and social circumstances present.

3 Ingold, T. (2013) *Making: Anthropology, Archaeology, Art and Architecture.* Routledge, p. I.
4 Gadamer, H. G. (1981) *Reason in the Age of Science*, p. 124.
5 Gans, Herbert J. (1962) *The Urban Villagers: Group and Class in the Life of* *Italian-Americans.* The Free Press, p. 12. Gans includes an appendix on the methods used in his study on p. 396.
6 Hamdi, N. (2004) *Small Change: About the Art of Practice and the Limits of Planning in Cities.* Earthscan, p. XXII.

Team meeting during fieldwork in Chicala, Luanda, coordinated by Paulo Moreira. © Kota 50, 2012

2.   Collaborative fieldwork

Initial experiences and contacts with a particular neighbourhood may be followed by a period of analysis, interpretation, and preparation of further site visits and project opportunities. Institutional collaborations with local architectural schools may be established, involving activities such as workshops. The methodologies employed in these workshops can mobilise many constituent parts of the neighbourhood's complex fabric: local authorities supporting our work, residents consenting to recount their lives and show us their houses, and students documenting their experiences and empathising with the population. The workshops may also serve to garner interest in the project among students and tutors.

Institutions may be willing to participate in university extension projects of this kind due to two main factors. On the one hand, presentations of previous experiences can make it clear that the issues raised by the project are rarely touched upon or discussed at local architecture schools. Tutors with a genuine interest in this area of architecture may view our collaboration as an opportunity to motivate students. On the other hand, the visibility conferred upon the project by exhibitions, publications, media coverage, and so on can attract institutional support and encourage the organisation of further workshops with expanded objectives.

The material produced during these workshops may include social data, spatial surveys, and design proposals, which provide relevant material for further study or for producing drawings, maps, images, and tables. In some cases, collaborative fieldwork may be viewed as a novel approach to research in the context of "critical neighbourhoods", unlike the more commonly used "passive" methods used by architects and researchers working in or on such places. Our approach to fieldwork is based on human involvement, testing the limits of collaboration among participants and residents.

Fieldwork methods should reflect the approach suggested by scholars in a variety of contexts. Nabeel Hamdi states that on-site participatory programmes can attract interest from the wider community and provide a better way to collect, analyse, and interpret information. Hamdi's words are straight to the point:

This kind of knowing is less normative, less easy to standardise in its routines and procedures, less tolerant of data-hungry study, and less reliant on statistics or systems analysis. (…) Instead, approximation and serendipity are the norm – the search for scientific precision is displaced in favour of informed improvisations, practical wisdom, integrated thinking and a good judgement based on a shared sense of justice and equity, and on common sense.[6]

The solidarity so commonly fomented by the workshops among institutions both within and beyond the neighbourhood points to the potential for symbiosis between a neighbourhood and its city. However, collaborative work in contested neighbourhoods is not limited to workshops with students and residents. Collaboration may also emerge from interactions with and between local professionals and artisans. In all cases, collaborative work must be ethically sound as a vehicle for dialogue and everyone involved in the project must be credited. Due to their nature as outsiders, however, architects will inevitably draw greater attention from the media and public institutions than students or artisans in the neighbourhood. Increasing exposure is undoubtedly one of the main contributions of any architectural project.

3. Institution building

During field trips, links can be established with local institutions. Workshops and presentations of the ongoing project in local academic and cultural circles will help strengthen collaboration. The workshops may result in publications compiling contributions from researchers and professionals who are accompanying the workshops or are familiar with the case study in some way. These books can be a useful tool for building closer relationships with local academic and professional institutions. They can also enhance the visibility of the site (and the project itself), as well as attracting support for the project in the local context in the form of funding opportunities and partnerships. Building partnerships is a step towards ensuring that work continues once the "experts" have gone.

There may be concern that partnerships with local public or private organisations can lead to a loss of independence and autonomy. Would a local institution agree to fund a study or project that critiques official urban policy? Would it be viable to receive public funding and institutional support to record and reveal the urban culture of a neighbourhood condemned to oblivion? Could some aspect of these projects be seen as a form of insurgence against the academic or political establishment?

In some contexts, engaging in or with "critical neighbourhoods" can be complex and such concerns are legitimate. In these cases, it is essential that unconditional institutional support is in place to ensure that the project carves out a space for itself and achieves its proposed objectives.

Research projects can be expressly designed to be inclusive and empowering, echoing similar methods in academic and civic spheres. The idea of "observatories" or "urban labs" is one potentially relevant model. These community-focused institutions bring a range of partners to work together, including local universities, NGOs, civil society groups, local authorities, and cultural institutions.

In *Housing by People*, John Turner presents four proposals for community engagement in contested communities, which are intended to enhance collaboration and communication between people. Turner's first two proposals are particularly relevant:

Proposal One is to set up an international communication network in order to intensify the use of existing channels of communication (both formal and informal) in ways that increase universal access and reduce the risks of exploitation by centralising powers.[7]

Here, Turner identifies case studies as the most pressing need. He recommends avoiding over-simplistic data compilation, which tends to be counterproductive as users are often undiscriminating and fail to distinguish data from information. This is supplemented by Turner's second proposal:

Proposal Two (...) is to set up a number of centres where case materials will be collected, indexed and made available to those needing access to the precedent sets. All such centres will be interconnected so that anyone can search the rest for particular documents or topics.[8]

Turner suggests a very simple idea: creating a publicly accessible archive. This could allow surveys of "critical neighbourhoods" to be presented in open-access, interrelated formats, including physical archives, digital archives, exhibitions, video/documentaries, books, etc.

Another advantage of this approach is that it supplies the financial resources needed to pursue the project at full speed, providing money to cover costs such as materials, student bursaries, or a publication. Archives are a meaningful way of responding to the struggles of contested communities. They may also serve to promote or mediate relationships across different civic and institutional jurisdictions (top-down and bottom-up) that were previously non-existent.

However, as in any project based in an institutional environment, these initiatives are often subject to burdensome, sometimes restrictive, bureaucratic and formal obligations. The hours spent on these formalities open up paths that would otherwise have

Bairro do Leal Appropriation, workshop with residents, neighbours, and participants (10 to 17 July 2021), coordinated by Paulo Moreira, organised by INSTITUTO, Porto. © INSTITUTO

remained closed. For example, they may enable information-sharing partnerships to be established with urbanism and planning departments.

To some degree, these factors point to a dimension of the work that transcends the purely academic or disciplinary to become a practical and political experiment. Above all, these research models are based on a methodology of direct involvement and engagement. The materials produced for the project will enable interaction between the participants themselves and between the participants and the settings in which they operate.

7 Turner, J. (1976) *Housing by People: Towards Autonomy in Building Environments*. Marion Boyars, p. 156.
8 Ibid., pp. 157–158.

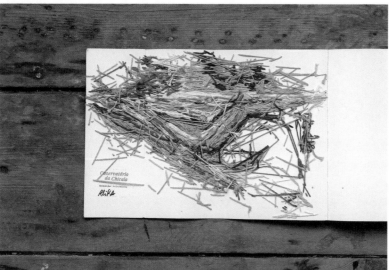

Making the Chicala Observatory book, a participatory project in collaboration with This is Pacifica. The book was coordinated by Paulo Moreira and Isabel Martins at Agostinho Neto University, Luanda. © Paulo Moreira, 2015

4. Archival research

The intention behind archival research is to recover positive memories that allow us to question why things came to be as they are and how they could be otherwise. This method enables a broad understanding of a neighbourhood's history. Public and private archives can provide relevant materials to broaden the scope of a literature review or inspire creative, unorthodox ways of engaging with the past. Archival research can be used to develop visual methods for representing the tensions inherent in any neighbourhood or city and the evolution of living conditions over time.

This type of research can also draw on materials from diffuse, private collections that were once hidden from public view, such as photographs of the research site at different times in its history. Archival records convey histories that may not be adequately captured by conventional (modernist) narratives, helping to "join the dots" of previously untold stories. In this way, historical research serves as an account of the collective production of the present. It is important to emphasise the significance of presenting plural versions of history "from below" and "from within", moving beyond official narratives.

Luis Damião analysing his father's photographic archive in Chicala, Luanda. © Paulo Moreira, 2021

5. Interpretative modes of representation

One of the driving forces behind research in "critical neighbourhoods" is the desire to portray urban conflicts in the neighbourhood/city relationship in a visual form. Gathering different types of information, knowledge, and data and using them to develop a visual understanding of a given subject is an act of practical research. Drawings, therefore, are presented as experimental hermeneutical representations rather than "flows of information".

The material collected should not simply be transformed into quantitative data, which would fall short in terms of grasping the site's true qualities and meaning due to its tendency to flatten vital urban situations into a certain statistical uniformity. On the contrary, quantitative information (tables and graphs) may only be relevant in the sense that it casts light on alternative ways of representing the city. Only with robust information about a place can we seriously explore what is taking place there. In this approach, the role of architects and researchers is to collect data and create ways of reorganising and representing the knowledge gleaned using architectural tools. By editing and interpreting the material, new insights on the subject in question begin to emerge.

Visuals and texts become reciprocal elements, offering different yet complementary pathways towards improved understanding of the subject. Visual representation holds great investigative potential: for instance, maps bring a degree of visibility to urban conflicts that is difficult to grasp from text alone, offer additional ways of probing beneath the surface of these disputes, and, at their best, indicate where borders can be bridged and plurality regained.

One of the most common methods for expressing the "larger forces" that shape any architectural study is mapping. This can be a rather challenging enterprise, as historical maps tend to underrepresent contested communities and territories. A nuanced reading of archival material and editing of historical records can make an important contribution to urban studies in "critical neighbourhoods", as well as to the architecture discipline and spatial practices more broadly.

Archival research becomes what Chris Perkins terms "critical cartography", a practical tool enabling relations that are inaccessible to disciplines such as human or urban geography.[9] Whereas an historian might comment upon an incomplete map or seek to reconstruct a misplaced past, a critically practising architect is able to intervene by producing spatial evidence or mapping real places to reveal once-obscured relations. This type of intervention may come to represent a regenerative form of practice, bringing different kinds of social, theoretical, and political struggle to the fore and allowing present and future forms of urban conflict to be interrogated.

Interpretative modes of visual representation open up new possibilities for knowledge generation. This may be one of architectural research's main contributions: to depict an underrepresented part of a city using practical methods. Drawings, graphs, and maps can be used to illustrate the site's spatial and urban order and reveal its interconnections with the wider context.

[9] Perkins, C. (2017) "Critical Cartography", in Kent, A.J. & Vujakovic, P. (eds.) *The Routledge Handbook of Mapping and Cartography*. Routledge.

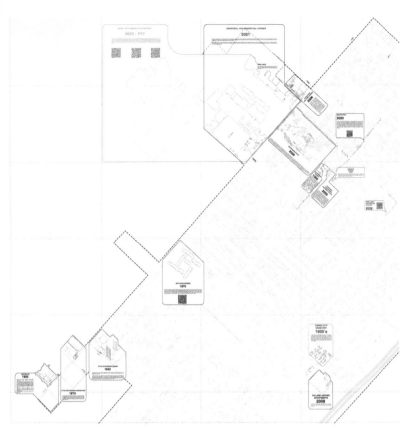

Map of Little Haiti, part of the Space for Everyone project led by Elisa Silva at
FIU – Florida International University in Miami. © Drawn by Ramses Allende, Fernando
Arana, Jose Arroyo, John Correa, and Jennyfer Hernandez, 2021

Point cloud photogrammetry of Monte Xisto, Matosinhos.
© Paulo Moreira and Prompt Collective, 2016

Jamaika is Portugal, Too public programme at maat, Lisbon.
© Interactive Brands Agency, courtesy of Fundação EDP, 2021

Model of Jamaika (2021), a collaborative work by Paulo Moreira,
with Chão – Oficina de Etnografia Urbana and José Sarmento Matos,
presented at maat in the the exhibition *X is Not a Small Country*
(18 March to 6 Sept. 2021), curated by Aric Chen, with Martina Muzi.
© Ivo Tavares

6. Public celebration

During any collaborative project, it will become clear that the more public and official the project becomes, the more dialogue it enables, the more research opportunities it generates, and the more bridges it builds. Therefore, part of our methodological approach should focus on raising awareness of the case study in contexts where it is typically unknown or unrecognised, both within and beyond the city in question.

This strategy is likely to be one of the primary vehicles for obtaining insight into the research topic. Firstly, the project can be widely presented in academic and specialist arenas. These events can offer valuable benefits and inputs, especially when it comes to feedback and connections they facilitate. Secondly, studying an urban configuration is in itself a balance between objective distance and immediate participation, requiring a mixed approach. Outcomes from conventional architectural methods and scholarly research can be complemented by a variety of practices at both the local and international levels. These can include pop-up installations, prototypes, exhibitions, videos, and performances, which bring the project to life, facilitate learning, and create the ideal conditions for others to understand the issues at hand.

Sometimes viewed as a "side effect" of a project, media coverage can be consciously used as part of a strategy to confer recognition upon the given neighbourhood, providing a vehicle to connect the site to the outside world and vice versa. Mobilising the media to report on the neighbourhood and/or design project may also be considered an act of empowerment and resistance. Marshall Berman would agree with the impact of such actions – after all, he acknowledged the role of media attention in making a neighbourhood visible:

What if the Bronxites of the 1950s had possessed the conceptual tools, the vocabulary, the widespread public sympathy, the flair for publicity and mass mobilisation that residents of many American neighbourhoods would acquire in the 1960s?[10]

Events organised in relation to a project are far from discrete and each one informs the project in some way. Conferences and discussions with individuals and professional bodies can provide evidence of general attitudes to the topic among the city's dominant classes. The more exposure received by the project, the more instructive the reactions it causes become. Participants in the project should be publicly acknowledged for their role in the process in different ways. Architects are encouraged to organise public events at which participants receive recognition for their efforts and the city is invited to celebrate the neighbourhood's culture through music, documentaries, exhibitions, music, and so on.

10 **Berman, Marshall [2010 (1982)]**, *All That is Solid Melts Into Air*, London and New York: Verso, p. 326.

7. Dissident practice

Beyond the institutional liaisons and platforms of visibility inherent to architectural practice in segregated neighbourhoods lies a more silent yet equally important dimension of the methodological approach. Documenting the dismantling of a neighbourhood and helping to "preserve" it in the face of different forms of violence inevitably involves listening to and connecting with the dissenting voices operating in and around the case.

An important component of the fieldwork can consist of finding and approaching these critical voices, which may come from local NGOs, human rights organisations, and (secret) activist groups. Sympathy with these resistance movements on the part of the architect does not entail the adoption of confrontational tactics or active engagement against the hegemonic forces of domination (official authorities or corporate groups). Yet neither does it mean taking a stance of self-conscious inefficacy and evasion. In other words, "doing nothing" in a situation of social injustice may be a self-defeating strategy.

The distinction between being a socially conscious architect and an activist or dissident is not clear-cut. In complex urban situations, these practices are often intertwined. As Ines Weizman explains in *Architecture and the Paradox of Dissidence*, "architecture is perhaps the least likely of practices to articulate a dissident position", as the practice of producing buildings "requires political powers that control the two main conditions necessary for construction to occur – land and money"[11]. While a "building" is not always the ultimate outcome of these projects, they may be framed within largely conservative institutional contexts.

The approach to be adopted by architects and researchers that is endorsed here involves articulating resistance to institutional and conventional practice in order to develop resilient projects. The "dissident practice" embedded in such projects seeks to expand the role of architects and researchers in critical spatial practice. While the discipline appears to be complicit in state and corporate disenfranchisement of the urban poor, these discreet (or undetectable) gestures and actions from "below" can offer a broader understanding of a particular urban conflict. These practices tend to elude detection and identification on the ground, but they are implicit in the technical language used in architecture.

11 Weizman, Ines (ed.) (2014), *Architecture and the Paradox of Dissidence*, Oxon: Routledge, p. 6.
12 The archive, which consists of more than 1.000 analogic photo films from 1975–2005, is currently held at INSTITUTO and is slowly being organised, examined, and digitalised by an interdisciplinary team, including paulo moreira architectures and visual anthropologist Inês Ponte, in close collaboration with the Damião family.

Case studies and contributions

In recent years, a growing number of architects and spatial practitioners have begun to act on their commitment to the idea that contested communities are here to stay and require selective intervention in order to achieve better living conditions. This book aims to contribute to the development of new approaches to so-called "critical" or "informal" neighbourhoods in the architectural field. It is inspired by doctoral and post-doctoral research into the reciprocal relationship between a neighbourhood and its wider city: Chicala, Luanda (Angola, Africa). To some degree, I was motivated to produce this publication by the fact that I did not want to look back on my PhD as something I did in the past or to publish it as a book as if shelving the whole process. I wanted my research to continue. The case study gave rise to a dialogue with other recent practical actions on different continents: La Palomera (Caracas, Venezuela, America), studied by Elisa Silva, and T Camp (Delhi, India, Asia), explored by Julia King.

The case of Chicala is framed by the conflicts arising amid Luanda's recent urban densification and its sociopolitical management. The neighbourhood's specific geographical location, integrity, and evolution made it vulnerable to colonial invasions and, more recently, to aggressive urbanism and large-scale masterplans. Despite this, the process of self-built development in Chicala has been largely neglected in research circles.

The first chapter aims to write Luanda's urban history afresh by foregrounding Chicala's contribution to the city. Taking a historical approach, an archive with artistic and transformative value is created to document the unique characteristics of a neighbourhood on the brink of extinction. The site's long history of natural formation and inhabitation is illustrated by photographs by Paulino Damião, known as Kota 50. Kota 50, who passed away in 2020, lived in Chicala for more than thirty years and used the neighbourhood as a base for documenting life in Angola. His personal and professional life intertwines with key moments in the country's history to produce a rare body of work.

Kota 50's archive offers a wealth of material for research into the history of Angola, as well as artistic and archival practices in photography. Drawing on his archive, we have built synergies with Damião's sons, Lino Damião and Luis Damião, via artistic projects revolving around residencies, workshops, and exhibitions.[12] To supplement their father's photographs, the chapter on Chicala concludes with first-hand accounts from Luis Damião and Lino Damião with fellow resident Nelo Teixeira, which reveal the collective effort involved in building the neighbourhood. Although Chicala's fate cannot be changed, this work reflects other ways in which architects can operate in complex urban settings.

La Palomera and T Camp, which are presented by fellow architects Elisa Silva and Julia King respectively, establish a dialogue with the Chicala case study, addressing the role of infrastructure, public space, and community engagement in these neighbourhoods. As well as these positive aspects, both contributions also consider how conflict can be instructive and important in boosting voice.

The second chapter discusses La Palomera, a neighbourhood in Caracas that continues to experience social segregation despite its vitality. Through a series of projects and activities, Elisa Silva shows that this is a viable urban place that deserves to be recognised as part of the city. Her chapter presents examples that show how design can help contest fragmented notions of the city. Designing built projects for the public space, implementing interdisciplinary educational and cultural programmes, organising celebrations, setting up art-based projects, conducting participatory mapping exercises, holding exhibitions, promoting door-to-door waste collection, activating derelict buildings for collective use… These actions, projects, and interventions all provide opportunities to enhance social capital. The work coordinated by Elisa Silva and Enlace Arquitectura has the potential to redefine perceptions of boundaries within the city.

In the third chapter, Julia King explores the material and social dimensions of infrastructure. T Camp, the smallest of the three neighbourhoods addressed in this book, illustrates the potential of incremental, small-scale improvements and expansions, suggesting that interventions of this kind can stitch the city together. The "failed" nature of this project (it was never implemented) points to the disconnect between informal processes and formal providers. Sometimes, good intentions can

Meeting between Paulo Moreira, Elisa Silva, and Julia King at Paulo Moreira's studio, Porto, 24 March 2021. © Valter Vinagre

be out of sync with demand for rapid urban change, as seen in New Delhi.

Public disinvestment and neglect emerge as a common feature in these three neighbourhoods. By analysing their unique characteristics, we engage in a rich professional and cultural exchange. We raise questions as to the role of architectural practice and research in contemporary societies, promoting engagement with complex social and urban situations by architects. The three case studies cast light on the impacts of bitter conflict between economy-driven urban policies and struggling contested communities.

The chapters addressing Chicala, La Palomera, and T Camp are followed by two closing texts. When discussing our projects and working methods, it became clear that the book would benefit from additional thoughts beyond the three case studies, as well as from "external" perspectives. We invited Matthew Barac to moderate a dialogue between the three authors: Julia King, Elisa Silva, and myself; and Ines Weizman to reflect on the role of architects as "critical" spatial practitioners.

This publication draws on the motif of "micro-processes" as a viable way of practising architecture in neighbourhoods that are silenced, excluded, or facing demolition. We hope that it will contribute to questioning the conventional relationship between architectural practice and research, and between academic and sociopolitical structures. Exploring a central component of architectural and urban reciprocity, this study aims to demonstrate that the city is capable of empowering and including people and their neighbourhoods, rather than excluding them.

Chicala

Why Chicala?

The decision to work in Chicala was taken shortly before plans for the complete erasure of the site were implemented and local authorities and private investors forcefully displaced its inhabitants to remote settlements with unsuitable living conditions. It became urgent to document and understand the urban form of this neighbourhood before it disappeared. Chicala affords an opportunity for in-depth reflection on the potential role of research in relation to complex urban situations, in particular those involving disappearing communities. This neighbourhood quite literally vanished before my eyes – the question here concerns the means of documentation and the methods employed in the unique observations and actions undertaken on the ground.

Paulo Moreira

Documenting a Disappearing Neighbourhood

This chapter is illustrated with photographs by Angolan photojournalist Kota 50 (unless credited otherwise). Kota 50 moved to Chicala with his family in the mid-1980s and portrayed everyday life in the neighbourhood at that time. The photographs are supplemented by first-hand accounts from his two sons, Lino Damião and Luis Damião.

Shifting ground

The Luandan littoral is constantly shifting. Major territorial changes are taking place in the Ilha de Luanda, where Chicala and other neighbourhoods are located. Records through the ages show that the area was a much longer and wider *restinga* (a sandy ridge, isthmus, or sandbank) in the sixteenth and seventeenth centuries than in the twentieth and twenty-first. *Restingas* are a common feature of Angola's coastline. They take the form of barrier islands or peninsulas created by sandbars, debris, and sediment, which form lagoons.

In Luanda, the *restinga* is commonly known as the Ilha de Luanda, the Ilha do Cabo, or simply the Ilha (island). It is primarily formed by the natural deposition of sands displaced by the currents of the Kwanza River (75 km south of Luanda), or eroded from the southern cliffs and redistributed by longshore currents in the ocean. Luanda's *restinga* has maintained a very low level of land and sand rising just a few metres from sea level.

The Ilha's morphological and sedimentary variation over the centuries is particularly extreme. Existing records are insufficient to fully understand its early configuration, making it difficult to trace an analytical history. Not only is there a lack of historical maps, but even the written descriptions available offer very different versions of the facts. The area's volatility largely derives from natural phenomena, from a constant battle between water and land. It was only in the twentieth century that consistent attempts were made to stabilise the shifting ground of the Ilha de Luanda. As yet, these actions have not been entirely successful.

While uncertainty surrounding parts of the Ilha coastal protection strategy remains, informal neighbourhoods are the subject of large-scale, long-term sanitising projects often too ambitious to be implemented. Despite these circumstances, many neighbourhoods continue to develop and mature informally. Chicala is one of the Ilha's oldest and most consolidated neighbourhoods, but its future is unknown. Regardless of its destiny, the settlement has made an undeniable contribution to the history of the city.

pp. 36–37 Partial demolition of Chicala,
Luanda. © Nadia Righele, 2014

The concrete cubes used for the protection spurs can be seen in the background along Luanda's coastline. The blocks were made at Hidroportos in Chicala, whose cement silos are among the neighbourhood's main landmarks. **Luis Damião**

This is the view from an area of the neighbourhood
that we used to call Jamaica. It was frequented
by artists, the first place where people saw others
smoking *liamba* and young people with dreadlocks...
It's known as Jamaica to this day. **Lino Damião**

Early inhabitation

The area where Chicala is located, as well as the Ilha de Luanda more broadly, has been inhabited since long before records began. The population that originally settled there were known as the Axiluanda (or Muxiluanda, in the plural). The toponymy of Axiluanda means "throwers of nets", as in "fishermen". The name of the city, Luanda, thus derives from the community living around Chicala and the Ilha.

Many questions remain unanswered regarding the initial settlement of the Axiluanda on the Ilha. It is not known whether the early population arrived on the Ilha via the *restinga* in Mussulo on their way north, or whether they travelled directly to the Ilha de Luanda using *jindóngo* (canoes) to make the crossing. The first hypothesis is viewed as more plausible due to the ease with which the first inhabitants, coming from the Kwanza River, would have found a route inland via the sea.

Over time, the N'dongo, who came from the Kingdom of N'gola on the mainland, joined the Axiluanda. Later, the Ilha de Luanda would be conquered and annexed to the Kingdom of Kongo, whose king lived further away to the north. The new inhabitants merged with the former two ethnic groups, the majority of the N'dongo having left the Ilha and settled on the mainland. The Ilha de Luanda was thus the stage for a process of miscegenation which continues today: historically, the site's formation and expansion were the result of continual migratory movements, with their attendant troubles and disruptions.

There is scattered information on the early inhabitation of the Ilha
de Luanda, describing the various initial *sanzalas* (settlements).
The population of the Ilha is known to have settled in small, scattered
settlements. With minor spelling variations, a common list of places is:
Felete, Mbelela, Tundo, and Mbimbi, all of which may have disappeared
as a result of the *kalembas* (ocean storms).[1] A number of texts and maps
on the formation of the *restinga* make reference to Chicala. Xikala
(*kimbundu* for Chicala) roughly translates to "the land that remained",
which is most likely a reference to the endurance of this stretch of
land despite the ocean's currents.[2] A sense of resistance to external
forces has always been part of the neighbourhood's essence.

1 See Carvalho, R. D. (1989) *Ana a Manda –*
Os Filhos da Rede. Lisbon: Instituto de
Investigação Científica Tropical, pp. 69–70
and Cardoso, C.A.L. (1972) *Os Axiluanda.*
Luanda: Culturang, p. 39.
2 *"Xi:* earth, contracted form of *ixi; kala:*
being, imperative of *kukala* = to be.

This is in Chicala 1, on the other side of the sea. The fishermen are hauling up their net. This fishing technique is known as *banga-banga*: they transport the net on the master's canoe, which can be seen in the background, and they leave two ends of the rope on land. This creates a full circle – on the photo you can just about see the other half – which is pulled by another group on the left. They'd pull on the net and then they'd come together here. Here, they're gathering up the nets and the canoe has arrived. They're holding the sinkers and the net is further back. It's a huge net. Finally, they wash it and hang it up to dry. **Luis Damião**

The women would wait for the men to bring in
the fish. The widows in Ilha and Samba used to cover
their entire faces and wear a kind of hat, which
was made from cardboard wrapped in black cloth
(as we found out later). They would spend one
or two years in mourning. Part of that time would be
at home, in the same room, and only then would
they start to go out into the street. They had a lot of
rituals. You don't see that much anymore.
Luis Damião

What the group of women on the sand are doing
is known as *saramuela* – preparing the small fry.
It's a technique where only the gills are removed.
Lino Damião

On the crossing, we'd sometimes use a rope for those who didn't know how to paddle. Or we'd go by boat. Here, they're leaving Chicala 1 for Chicala 2. In the background, you can see the fishermen's houses and above them are the large houses in the Cidade Alta. The man standing there, brother António, disappeared. Nobody ever found out what happened to him. **Luis Damião**

Postcolonial appropriation

Following Angola's independence from Portugal (1975), urban appropriation in Luanda blurred the distinctions between the "colonial city" and the so-called *musseques* or slums. Appropriation of former colonial quarters became a typical feature of postcolonial Luanda. The city was the scene of a diverse range of urban experiences, distinct from the traditional (racial and economic) dualisms that had marked the cityscape during the colonial period. It belonged to everyone, in a perpetual process of adjustment of modernist architecture to an evolving way of life. There were animals on the balconies of multistorey buildings, plantations in bath tubs, and families of ten to twelve people living in small apartments, who cooked on the floor, made bonfires with the parquet, and transformed lift shafts into dumps.

Luanda's vertical appropriation developed at the same time as the exponential horizontal expansion of the self-built *musseques*, due to the arrival of thousands of internally displaced migrants searching for security and economic prosperity in the capital. In the years following independence, despite the hasty exit of the Portuguese settlers, Luanda's population grew over 100%, from 500,000 to over 1 million people. The pace of growth continued over the years, reaching an estimated 8 million residents in 2021. Urban sprawl took hold in the absence of any formal planning: public networks became saturated, while water, power, and sewerage infrastructure proved insufficient and, in many cases, non-existent. The city evolved to become more complex. Informality became one of the city's most prominent characteristics.

In the post-independence period, which was characterised by constant novelty, the authorities sought to adapt in order to govern the city. Throughout 1975, the *Jornal de Angola* featured an almost daily section entitled *A Vida nos Bairros* (Life in the Neighbourhoods), a kind of tableau reporting on matters relating to each neighbourhood. From this period on, we can be certain that the term in official and common use was *bairro,* which does not convey the same pejorative connotation as *musseque* or "slum". The *musseques* became *bairros* in their own right. The city's postcolonial history may be told, therefore, from the neighbourhood level.

Page from *Jornal de Angola*, 24 Oct. 1975. Source: The British Library

"*A Vida nos Bairros*" provides evidence of the vibrant, complex collective movement that began to operate in the city of Luanda in the post-independence period. This intense period of self-organisation officially brought an end to the narrative of the *musseque* as a pathological site.

Chicala meets Angolan history

On 10 September 1979, Angola's first president, Agostinho Neto, died in Moscow. His rule had lasted only four years (1975–9). On Monday 17 September 1979, on what would have been his fifty-seventh birthday, Neto's funeral was held in Luanda. The ruling party MPLA announced that the body of their *Herói Nacional* (national hero) was to be preserved in a mausoleum, which would become the centrepiece of the political and administrative centre already planned in 1977. A drawing dated 11 October 1979, just three weeks after Neto's funeral, indicated that the mausoleum would be erected on the site of the Morro de Santa Bárbara, a hill near the coast.

The construction of the mausoleum had a major impact on the redevelopment of the surrounding areas, including the area known as Chicala 2 on the continental side (given its proximity to Chicala, on the insular side). As construction began, the earth removed from the Santa Bárbara hill was displaced to the natural sandbank that had started to form by the coast, opposite insular Chicala. The landfill began to raise the surface of the northern side of the natural sandbank which, at that point, was scattered with a few wooden houses inhabited by fishing families. Deciphering the topographic conditions of Chicala allows us to understand its reciprocal relationship with Angola's history.

The neighbourhood is surrounded by some of Luanda's main historical landmarks. As well as Agostinho Neto's Mausoleum (a post-independence monument), the São Miguel fortress (a colonial monument), the political and administrative centre (including the Presidential Palace and the National Assembly), and an iconic colonial church are only a short walk away from Chicala. By analysing this particular place and its surroundings, we glean an insight into the conditions and constituents that have influenced and shaped the city throughout history. Chicala serves as a laboratory for understanding the virtue or meaning of the reciprocity between informal neighbourhoods and the city of Luanda.

The fact that the site is bordered by such a symbolic context within the nation state inevitably calls for a historical and political interpretation of Chicala in relation to Luanda and Angola. The neighbourhood's geographical circumstances have had undeniable material consequences throughout the ages, with its strategic location giving rise to numerous conflicts and invasions. In this respect, Chicala is not an exception to the larger city: rather, it constitutes a microcosm of what the entirety of Luanda has been and could become. It embodies social and urban structures at different levels, along with significant aspects of the history of both the city and the country.

Chicala's ongoing clearance and suppression is but the most recent episode in a broader process of continual change: the wider area has been destroyed and rebuilt several times during the history of the city of Luanda. Yet, amid constant tension and uncertainty, despite the rejections, constraints, and erasures it experienced, the neighbourhood continued to develop and was able to flourish into a viable place for accommodating diverse ways of life, which had never been properly recorded or understood.

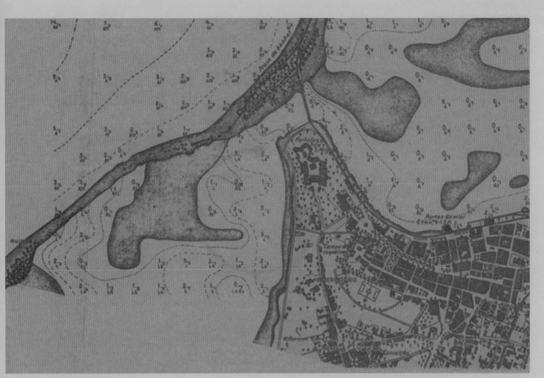

Plan of Luanda, 1937. Note the word "ruínas" (ruins) on the left, providing evidence of an old settlement. Source: Archive IICT

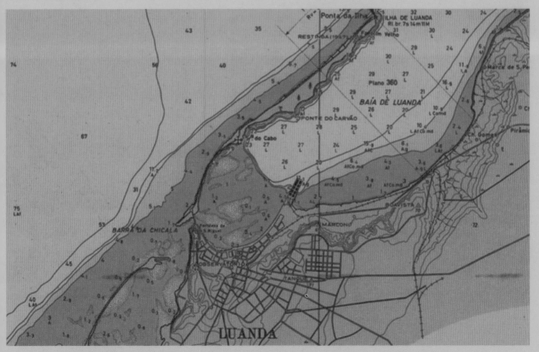

Plan of Luanda, 1964. By the middle of the twentieth century, the *kalembas* had caused entire sections of sand on the southern side of the island to disappear. The Chicala area had become cut off from the island (its long, thin configuration gave rise to the name Felete or fillet). Source: Archive IICT

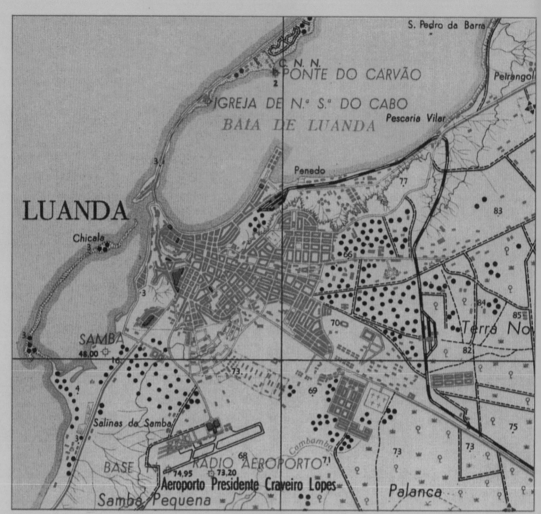

Plan of Luanda, 1960. Despite becoming separated from the Ilha in the mid-1950s, the settlement of Chicala has remained in place. Here, it is depicted as one of the relevant places named on the map. Source: *Atlas Geográfico* (1982), República Popular de Angola: Ministério da Educação, Vol.1, p. 7.

Portraying everyday life

Most of the houses in Chicala are examples of incremental building and the history of a single dwelling can represent the development of the entire neighbourhood over a given period. A house's evolution over time intertwines with the history of the family, the neighbourhood, and, arguably, the country as a whole. Chicala's social and urban order is the result of ongoing dialogue and negotiation between the private and the collective – the neighbourhood serves as a lens through which Luanda's urban history and development can be explored as a palimpsest of calculated and arbitrary manoeuvres.

Yet this chapter does not only aim to "fill the gap" and record a place due to disappear completely for the sake of posterity. To frame this research as a mere attempt to create an archive of the history of Chicala would be uncomfortably in line with the outside forces responsible for its very disappearance. The chapter instead focuses on a broader intellectual problem, a paradox that appears to reject Chicala and Luanda's informal settlements in all their cityness and fullness of life.

When the Damião family settled in Chicala in the mid-1980s, civil war was raging across the country. Hundreds of thousands of internally displaced people arrived in Luanda, fleeing the conflict that was severely affecting other provinces in the country. The photographs by Kota 50 (aka Paulino Damião) accompanying this chapter portray everyday life in the neighbourhood at that moment in time. His exhaustive exploration of Chicala from within raises questions as to Luanda's fundamental incoherence and unpredictability as an urban system where the virtues and significance of informal *bairros* are often overlooked.

That's our neighbour. When she bought a plot of land, they brought their wooden house here (they dismantled it and reassembled it; that was common in Chicala). The original houses in the neighbourhood were built that way, out of wood or straw mats or palm branches. You can see the concrete blocks for building the permanent house.
Lino Damião

Next to the house, there was a vacant lot known as *tandelas* – an area covered in shells, where the women would lay out the fish to dry. They let us store bricks there for a while before they were transported to our plot to build our house.
Lino Damião

This is the fence along the front of our house.
It was made from elements used on long-distance
routes to dig out lorries. The pillar is a bumper
from a lorry. That's Nanana, the eldest daughter
of a couple who took us in, mama N'Doma and
Tio Jorge. **Lino Damião**

This was a family gathering – a visit from our aunt and uncle, grilled rabbit. I'm there in the background looking for firewood. Lino's bringing the spices. People are sitting beneath the *jango*. Our dad planted the fig tree during Sam Nujoma's [President of Namibia] first visit to Angola. It was already big when he brought it from Parque Heróis de Chaves. Here you can see the clothes drying, towels, bedspreads... In May, the tide would reach those canes. **Luis Damião**

This *jango* used to face the other way. It was a carousel with a few rollers and chains, where the kids would play and spin. The circle at the top is an alloy wheel from a lorry. **Lino Damião**

At that time, Dad was doing a photography course with some Soviet teachers. He decided to stay in Chicala while the others went to the Baixa [downtown]. This is a posed shot with one of our cousins. That was our first year in Chicala. **Lino Damião**

Our house was built from all sorts of things: washing machines, bed frames, car body panels, lift doors... People called it "the iron palace". At low tide, you could walk several metres. When the tide came in, it entered our yard – we learnt to swim in the yard. Here, they'd already demolished the initial house. You can see the "teeth" for building the house next door, which belonged to Tio Neves. On the left, you can see an iron structure – it had a first floor to give shade. **Luis Damião**

Memories and spatial practices

Since our research into Chicala began in 2010, a series of collaborations with local artists and artisans have been set up to decipher the neighbourhood's spatial order and the nature of its reciprocal relationship with Luanda. These interdisciplinary projects are the product of diverse experiences in the fields of architecture and cultural production, and they foster dialogue and interaction between artistic practice, research, politics, and social issues.

As the founder and artistic director of INSTITUTO in Porto since 2018, I have established a series of cultural programmes featuring artists, curators, and researchers working between Angola and Portugal.[3] As part of this initiative, both Kota 50's sons Luis Damião and Lino Damião (with Nelo Teixeira, another former resident of Chicala) carried out artistic work at INSTITUTO based on their interpretation of historical or spatial aspects of Chicala at different times in 2021.[4]

Using installations, the artists were able to contribute to discussions of relevant issues concerning Chicala, Angola, and informal neighbourhoods more broadly. This work is based on a curatorial approach developed over the course of a decade. The findings of our lengthy investigation have allowed us to conceptualise spatial practices and create new forums, transcending the bounds of the profession to raise questions about historical and contemporary topics.

Chicala's fate is already sealed. However, the design, research, and curatorial practices arising from our study of the neighbourhood can offer other architects, urbanists, students, historians, and even policy makers more inclusive ways of approaching the discipline than those commonly discussed at architecture debates.

The intersection between cultural projects, research studies, and collaborative installations reflects a fondness for art, architecture, cities, and people, and a desire to further explore the reciprocal relationships between them. This is one of the main contributions that I believe we make as architects and citizens – expanding conventional notions of the role of architects to position them as negotiators and facilitators of local knowledge. Our projects can contribute to consolidating the "collective memory" of a place and point to possible paths for promoting the architectural potential of disappearing communities.

3 In 2018, I decided to create a more far-reaching project to extend and supplement my studio's activity. I founded INSTITUTO, a focal point for different forms of cultural expression, where we have been organising exhibitions, publications, talks, and workshops, as well as hosting residencies for artists and architects. Our programme transcends the field of architecture to encompass the visual and spatial arts, critical thinking, and multidisciplinary collaborations.
4 The residencies by Lino Damião and Nelo Teixeira at INSTITUTO took place at different times in 2021 with support from the Direção-Geral das Artes / Ministry of Culture of Portugal. This included an exhibition called *Kubanga Kukatula* (28 July to 3 Sept. 2021). Luis Damião's residency took place from 4 Aug. to 15 Oct. 2021, with support from InResidence (Ágora – Cultura e Desporto, E.M.). His residency was accompanied by an open studio titled *Arquivos* (17 Sept. to 15 Oct. 2021) and a workshop (15 Oct. 2021), where participants could interact with the artist and learn about his creative process.

Kubanga Kukatula (2021), by Lino Damião and Nelo Teixeira, presented at INSTITUTO
(28 July to 3 Sept. 2021), curated by Paulo Moreira. © Ivo Tavares

Alongside fellow artist Nelo Teixeira, Lino Damião
worked on an installation that recreates spatial
experiences of informality in Chicala. *Kubanga
Kukatula*, the title of the project, means "to assemble
and disassemble" in Kimbundu and refers to
Chicala's transitory nature, where architecture
and urban space are constantly made, unmade,
and remade as part of a collective effort.

Arquivos (2021), by Luis Damião, presented at INSTITUTO
(17 Sept. to 15 Oct. 2021), curated by Paulo Moreira. © Ivo Tavares

Luis Damião's work focuses on manipulating
and printing images from his father's extensive
photographic archive. In an exhibition titled
Arquivos, the artist researched, selected, edited,
and transformed material from the vast collection
to produce new works.

La Palomera

     CHAPTER TWO BY ELISA SILVA

Why La Palomera?

Our relationship with La Palomera began in 2016 when, together with the community, we transformed what had been a thirty-year-old, de-facto open-air waste collection area, into a lively public space. It became quickly apparent that La Palomera would be an amazing community to further experiment with the broader dynamics of urban integration. In 2018, we jointly promoted the "Integration Process Caracas" program, which hosted events, celebrations, dances, walks, bocce ball games, and exhibitions open to all audiences. Through the creation of a permanent cultural center fueled by the organization of a community-based NGO, this dynamic and democratic way of co-thinking the city will become further practiced and evolve into a shared-design of the city pertinent well beyond the limits of the barrio.

Elisa Silva

BARRIO IS CITY
Public Space, Art and Pedagogy as Tools for Urban Integration

The author decided to write
in her native American English.

La Palomera in Caracas, Venezuela, could be considered a critical neighborhood, if we understand critical as code for *barrio* or *favela*. It was built entirely by residents outside the protocols of conventional development. The first inhabitants settled in 1937, when the Nuestra Señora del Rosario church allowed workers to use part of the hill that is now La Palomera to grow vegetables and build homes.[1] As a result, the neighborhood is closely linked to the colonial town of Baruta, and is far older than the surrounding 1970s and 80s urban developments.

In spite of their longstanding presence, La Palomera and Caracas's other *barrios* are viewed as marginal outcasts. Like most self-built neighborhoods, services arrived in La Palomera gradually and are notably less efficient and dependable than elsewhere in Caracas. Yet there are many characteristics associated with *barrios,* including La Palomera, that are quite noteworthy. The neighborhood contains homes that are far larger, more comfortable, and more flexible than houses in other parts of the city. La Palomera is home to many professionals, including doctors, lawyers, and engineers, contesting the notion that it is a uniform agglomeration of poor, uneducated people. Violence and lack of personal security do not affect La Palomera any more or less than the rest of the city. Meanwhile, certain valuable features that are unique to the *barrio* represent an asset. The stairs and walkways are mostly pedestrian and cars are largely absent. Parents allow their children to play freely outside with other kids in the neighborhood, which is unheard of in Caracas's formal developments. In other words, despite its favorable or at least neutral urban conditions, the *barrio* continues to be stigmatized as different, other, inferior, and not part of the city.

How can design help contest this rather dysfunctional, fragmented conception of the city? How can *barrios* form part of the collectively acknowledged urban map? How can Caraqueños conceive a city that is complete and includes the *barrios*?

1 Flamerich, G.R. (12 May 2012) "Baruta: Un pueblo con su propio ritmo", Cátedra de periodismo UCAB.

pp. 68–69   Enlace Arquitectura and La Palomera team.
© Enlace Arquitectura, 2020

Public space

Between 2016 and 2018, Enlace Arquitectura worked with the community in La Palomera to construct two public spaces: one in the sector of *La Cruz* on a site that had previously been an open-air waste dump and the other in *Las Brisas* on what was once a car park. Although both experiences were a great success and were highly appreciated by residents, public space alone was not enough to encourage a more integrated urban experience. People from outside La Palomera would need to be invited to get to know the neighborhood and visit the new plazas, other urban spaces, look out points, stores, shops, and neighbors. Other strategies and disciplines needed to be engaged.

Art and pedagogy

Toward the end of 2018, Enlace Arquitectura and Ciudad Laboratorio launched an educational and cultural program in La Palomera titled "Integration Process Caracas". The program featured walks, activities, and celebrations that invited people to get to know La Palomera, as well as a manifesto and two exhibitions. On one level, these efforts challenged audiences to question their lingering discrimination of the *barrio* and its inhabitants, and to acknowledge it as part of the city. More importantly, alongside residents of La Palomera and a host of artists, journalists, educators, and other people interested in the project, they also helped crystalize urban narratives based on dialogue and shared interests between *barrio* and non-*barrio* residents. These narratives proved critical in creating a horizontal platform for exchanging knowledge – about gardening, traditional dances, or story-telling – where everyone participates as equals, without hierarchies, entitlements, or pity. This horizontal exchange models the tone and mentality that should govern discussions regarding the future of the city and the *process* in particular, with an emphasis on granting everyone an equal voice. The city's fragmentation will not be overcome by applying more of the same top-down "improvements" to the *barrio*, but rather through participatory engagement where everyone is invested in listening to and acknowledging the other. Urban integration is arguably much more the consequence of desire than of physical interventions. It is embraced in symbolic acts of recognition rather than philanthropic manifestations of good intentions.

Orthogonal plan of La Palomera - Caracas, Venezuela. © Aerea Studio & Miguel Salas, 2020

What can design do to help contest this rather dysfunctional and fragmented conception of the city? How can *barrios* enter the collective and acknowledged urban map? How can Caraqueños conceive a city that is complete and includes the barrios?

Plaza La Cruz, La Palomera – Caracas, Venezuela. © Enlace Arquitectura, 2016

This area of land in the sector known as La Cruz in
the *barrio* of La Palomera had served as a place
 to dump waste for over thirty years. As part of the
"City Planting" program funded by Citibank Venezuela,
it was transformed into a public space. Children
participated in the process by helping insert bottle
caps into the pavement and making a bench from
recycled pallets.

2 Williams, K. V. (2004)
"We Need Artists' Ways
of Doing Things: A Critical
Analysis of the Role of
the Artist in Regeneration
Practice", in Blundell
Jones, P., Till, J. & Petresco,
D. (eds.) *Architecture and
Participation*. Routledge.

3 Nussbaum, M. (2016)
*Not for Profit: Why
Democracy Needs the
Humanities*. Princeton.

Integration Process Caracas relied heavily on culture, art, and "the artists' way of doing things" because of their open-ended nature, their ability to engage people, and their unique effectiveness in provoking reflection.[2] This approach echoes the words of Martha Nussbaum in *Not for Profit: Why Democracy Needs the Humanitie*s, where she states that "the arts, by generating pleasure in connection with acts of subversion and cultural reflection, produce an enduring and even attractive dialogue with the prejudices of the past, rather than one fraught with fear and defensiveness".[3] The photographs below show some of the key events that shaped the program.

Mirador Las Brisas, La Palomera – Caracas, Venezuela. © Enlace Arquitectura, 2018

Las Brisas lies on the southern edge of the *barrio* La Palomera and is the highest point in the neighborhood. The playground site enjoys breathtaking views toward the city and the Avila Mountain, as well as a temperate climate characterized by a constant soft breeze. Enlace Arquitectura worked with the community, holding several open assemblies where ideas for transforming a parking lot were discussed.

Negotiations with vehicle owners were productive and the prime spot under the *Javillo* tree was designated to become a playground. The hexagonal swing structure defines the space, with five swings facing a central focal point so that people can see each other as they swing. There is also the potential to gradually transform the entire ridge along the southern edge of La Palomera into a larger linear park through further development.

Integration Process Caracas – "Art Pedagogy and the City". © Régulo Gómez, 2019

The Manifesto to the Complete City written by Cheo Carvajal was read in Plaza Baruta Bolívar by two well-known Venezuelan artists: Carlos Sánchez and Mariela Suárez. The manifesto is a call to recognize the *barrio* as part of the city.
Link: https://prodavinci.com/la-ciudad-completa/

Integration Process Caracas. © Enlace Arquitectura, 2019

The manifesto reading was followed by a walk
through the *barrio*, with stops along the way where
decimas (rhyming songs written specifically about
the *barrio*, celebrating its neighbors, traditions, and
culture) were sung by their composer José Pérez.

Integration Process Caracas began by launching an open call for artists to propose art-based projects that would engage the community. © Gabriel Nass, 2019

The projects selected from the open call included "Capsulas Culturales", where dancers from Ensayo Colectivo taught schoolchildren how to perform traditional Venezuelan dances. Another contemporary dance group and Laboratorio Ciudadano worked with the children from a soup kitchen, measuring their movement and bodies at different spatial scales to improve their self-awareness and self-confidence. A third group of artists taught high school students to make wood cuts of scenes in the *barrio* and tell their stories, which were then compiled into sewn, printed booklets. A fourth group mapped the gardens in La Palomera and interviewed their owners about the history of the garden, the plants they grew, and their recommendations on how to use, grow, and maintain the plants, many of which are edible or medicinal. They then gave a tour of the gardens in La Palomera, which was attended by outside guests including landscape architects and botanical experts. Each of these initiatives reached out to different groups within the *barrio* and allowed the project to connect with a more representative cross-section of its inhabitants.

Integration Process Caracas – "Ciudad Completa, Ciudad Desbordada". © Régulo Gómez, 2019

The fourth meeting held as part of the Integration Process Caracas program focused on recognizing the *barrio*'s open spaces, walkways, and stairs, as well as spaces such as the "bolas criollas" or bocce courts that are common in *barrio* communities. La Palomera has three such courts. Residents taught visitors how to play and a lively game ensued, celebrating access to a public space typology that is frequently present in *barrios* and could be enjoyed by all.

Integration Process Caracas – Cruz de Mayo and Mobile Museum. © Régulo Gómez, 2019

In our conversations with neighbors, we learned about the traditional celebration of the Cruz de Mayo in La Palomera, which had been prevented from taking place for twenty years due to economic hardship among the community. We decided to reinstate the celebration, following the traditional rituals but adding a large-scale model of the community and its surroundings, which was used in a procession from the Baruta town square into the *barrio*. There were also performances by members of the community, mostly children, who had participated in the artists' workshops. Large numbers of residents from La Palomera and people from the rest of the city participated in the event. This was an important turning point in our relationship with the community and in our understanding of how to move forward with the project, taking cues from the community and acknowledging the value in what they already have and do.

Fiesta de los Fundadores. © Régulo Gómez, 2019

The next event after the Cruz de Mayo was the Fiesta de los Fundadores, where the founding families of La Palomera and their descendants told stories of how La Palomera began. The event was very well attended by members of the community and outside guests. It was followed by music and *joropo*, a typical Venezuelan dance.

Ciudad Completa: La Palomera, Reconocimiento y Celebración exhibition.
Hacienda La Trinidad, Caracas, Venezuela. © Régulo Gómez, 2021

The events, walks, celebrations, manifestos, and mappings organized as part of the project were exhibited at Hacienda La Trinidad in Caracas last year. Under the title "The Complete City: La Palomera, Recognition and Celebration", the exhibition shared the wealth of knowledge and culture experienced in the community with audiences that included both the local inhabitants and anyone else in the city. The exhibition challenged common assumptions and asked visitors to begin to erode the stigma typically projected onto *barrios*.

The exhibition argued that people rather than institutions or governments define and can potentially redefine the perceived limits within the city. To integrate and suture the city, people's mental maps must be expanded, enhancing their knowledge and actively seeking to overcome a lack of fluidity and fragmentation in the city. This expansion is rewarded with the excitement of discovering new territories and communities, as demonstrated by the high levels of attendance at the events and repeat visits.

Part of the Integration Process Caracas experience was exhibited at the Corderie dell'Arsenale as part of the 17th International Architecture Exhibition – La Biennale di Venezia 2021. The exhibition featured the 260 species in the Ethnobotanical Dictionary of Plants from the Gardens of La Palomera, as well as a suspended 8-meter-long model of the walkways, stairs, public spaces, and gardens.

The 17th International Architecture Exhibition – La Biennale di Venezia 2021. "The Complete City: La Palomera, Recognition and Celebration", May 22 to Nov. 21, 2021. © Rafael Peña, 2021

The symbolic weight of equal services

Integration Process Caracas also paved the way for operational and physical transformations to take place. Waste is now collected door-to-door in La Palomera, bringing the quality of the service closer to that practiced in the rest of the city. Typically, in the *barrios*, waste is managed by simply leaving an open-air container along the edge of the closest road. People are expected to take their waste there themselves, resulting in a very unpleasant experience for the residents living near to the dump. The waste container greets everyone who enters the *barrio*, communicating the unfair notion that they are different, inferior, and less deserving of quality urban services. The door-to-door collection system now in place allows waste to be gathered by a team of employees who place it directly into the garbage trucks without the need for a permanent intermediary container. Once the system had been in place for a year, the container at the foot of Calle Salom was removed and a terraced garden was built and planted in its place with help from residents.

Calle Salom, before the planters. © Enlace Arquitectura, 2020

Calle Salom planters. © Enlace Arquitectura, 2020

The planters on Calle Salom in La Palomera represent the culmination of a door-to-door collection program begun in 2019 by Fospuca, a third-party waste collection company that works in the municipality of Baruta. Waste is now collected door-to-door, just like everywhere else in the city, by a group of workers who are in many ways re-enacting a service once performed by the *mochileros* or backpackers, who would carry the waste in bags on their backs, as older generations in the *barrio* will remember. Once the system had been operative for several months, we were finally able to dispense with the open-air waste container that had sat at the foot of the *barrio* for decades and replace it with planters. These are now overflowing with plants, some of which were donated by members of the community.

Modeling a democratic city-making process

We are also actively working to transform the abandoned space in the Casa de Todos Annex, where a key event in the Integration Process Caracas program took place in October 2019: "Nothing Out of the Ordinary". The structure is a half-ruined, half-finished house that had been shut up for several decades. William Diaz, a resident of La Palomera, showed it to us and asked what could be done there. The invitation was an important display of trust. Aware of the scarcity of space in the *barrio,* we understood it was almost criminal for the house to remain abandoned.

The Casa de Todos Annex has grown out of what is already there. Each iteration or phase emerges from the previous one and is grafted onto the existing building in some way. As construction progresses, residents are invited to participate in each stage, curing bamboo to use for the roof structure or learning how to collect rainwater for domestic purposes using the Annex' harvesting system. The process itself is designed to be inclusive and to model shared participation. The Annex is a hybrid structure that speaks to the *barrio*'s traditional building culture, where structures grow progressively and nothing is ever truly finished. The design synthesizes the knowledge and experiences of many, drawing on multiple, simultaneous layers through a prolonged curatorial process.

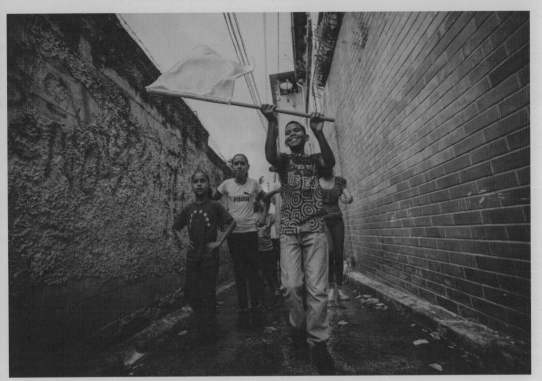

"Nothing Out of the Ordinary". © Régulo Gómez, 2019

In conversations with our team, we decided to organize a large celebration to showcase cultural groups from La Palomera and the Integration Process Caracas program. The event was held at the Casa de Todos Annex, which is conveniently positioned at the intersection between the town of Baruta and the *barrio* of La Palomera. Both our team and residents cleaned up the house, then two doors were opened to allow access from the street. The fiesta began with a procession from Plaza Bolivar in Baruta, led by the dance group Ensayo Colectivo, and the children who had learned to dance with them at previous workshops. They led and welcomed everyone into the Annex building and the celebration continued indoors.

"Nothing Out of the Ordinary". © Régulo Gómez, 2019

A contemporary dance group that had worked with the soup kitchen children at another set of workshops performed a dance on the second floor and asked the audience to follow them. There were video screenings by artists and several music groups from La Palomera and Fundación Bigott played new and traditional music in many different styles. Guests could purchase *sancocho* (a Venezuelan stew) and beer. Children of all shapes, colors, and sizes, living in the *barrio* and in other parts of the city, formed a train and weaved through the crowd. The music lasted for hours. It was a truly magical day that no one wanted to see end, leaving everyone with the hope that the space would become a permanently active part of the *barrio*.

"Nothing Out of the Ordinary". © Régulo Gómez, 2019

The project will always be incomplete and open to further additions and alterations, making it inclusive both in concept and practice. Incompletion evokes movement, perpetual transformation, refinement, and revision. It encourages and is ready to receive contributions, so that anyone and everyone feels invited to engage in the process. In his article "From Object to Field" (1997), Stan Allen offers a discursive tool for thinking about this open-ended process:

> *Field conditions and logistics of context reassert the potential of the whole, not bounded and complete (hierarchically ordered and closed), but capable of permutation: open to time and only provisionally stable. They recognize that the whole of the city is not given all at once. Consisting of multiplicities and collectivities, its parts and pieces are remnants of lost orders or fragments of never-realized totalities. Architecture needs to learn to manage this complexity, which, paradoxically, it can only do by giving up some measure of control.*[4]

Authorship is a moot point in the Casa de Todos Annex, superseded by the intention for it to remain mutable, as a surface where people can both leave and find their mark in space. The Casa de Todos Annex is in the process of becoming La Palomera Center for Art and Culture, with a year-round program of activities for people from the community and the rest of the city. The program combines tradition and modernity: *diablos danzantes* rehearsals and theater productions, a cooking school, and gardening lessons. Its hybrid nature reflects the very essence of Latin American culture, as described by Nestor García Canclini in *Hybrid Cultures: Strategies for Entering and Leaving Modernity* (2005). Hybridity has the virtue of evading judgement by being both/and instead of either/or.

4 Allen, S. (1997) "From Object to Field", *Architectural Design*, 67, p. 31.

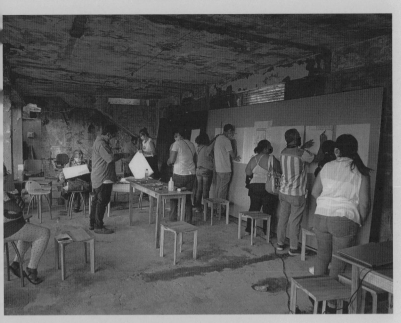

Transformation of the Casa de Todos Annex.
© Enlace Arquitectura, January 2020 – ongoing

Transformation of the Casa de Todos Annex.
© Enlace Arquitectura, January 2020 – ongoing

When the Integration Process Caracas program ended, our attention turned to the Annex and its potential to become a cultural center closely tied to the community in La Palomera. Several construction phases have been established, identifying key components that could be opened to wider participation. The hope is that this dynamic process will provide a model of what integration might look like, even if only on a small scale.

Funding for the transformation process and the organization's structure was secured from the Swiss Embassy in Venezuela and the PISSCA fund from the French Embassy in Venezuela, together with Cauce A.C, as well as the Graham Foundation in Chicago and Across Design in Munich.

The space will be run by an NGO modeled on other cultural organizations in Latin America that we interviewed during the summer of 2020. A long-term lease has been secured from the municipal council.

We asked the community to propose or present activities for the space and identified several music groups, a youth choir, and a theatre group called Getsemani, which had been operating in La Palomera for 13 years. Getsamani performed a play on January 31, 2020 and are thrilled at the idea of having a permanent stage. A martial arts initiative is also keen to use the space, as is the group that rehearses the Diablos Danzantes. A cooking school will open on the second floor once the kitchen is completed, which we hope will be run by the school currently working from Calixto Perez's house just a few blocks away. We are all keen on encouraging William, a talented gardener with extensive knowledge of planting and harvesting, to teach gardening to enthusiasts and anyone interested in learning, using the courtyard space.

The project maintains the building's existing structure as much as possible. Three elements have been added: a restroom, stairs to connect the floors, and a roof structure over the second floor. The underside of the roof has been lined with bamboo, which was processed at a workshop taught by Gabriel Nass and attended by many people from the community.

Lastly, rainwater is collected from the roof and channeled into a cistern that supplies water to the kitchen and restrooms. Access to water in Caracas and in Venezuela more broadly is highly problematic. Service quality has been severely affected over the years, so the project will not only provide the Annex with a secure water source (located in the tropical belt, Caracas receives copious rainfall practically throughout the year) but also serve as a model for families to replicate in their own homes.

Concluding thoughts

The Integration Process Caracas program and the transformation of the Annex attempt to contribute to the discourse in Venezuela and beyond on how to promote a more integrated city. The *how* is certainly much more important than the *what*. Just as John Turner's *Housing by People: Towards Autonomy in Building Environments* (1976) argues that housing must be understood as a verb, so too are architecture, design, and the public realm capable of yielding far more when the *how* is considered. Understanding the process of the project's conception, construction, and management as a prolonged rehearsal, can lead to the enactment of a space more fully charged with its potential to acknowledge, integrate, and even reconcile the plurality of people comprising urban life.

In this sense, a democratic design process is being modeled in the La Palomera Center for Art and Culture. It points to the humility and open-mindedness of designers to operate with less control, with an interest in drawing over the traces of what already exists and advocating for systems that are hybrid, grafted, and always in the process of completion. Projected on a larger scale, this process begins to model how an integrated city might be formed and operate.

n *Gender Trouble* (1990), Judith Butler makes a proposal that refers to
ssues of gender but is equally valid for the subjective labels assigned
o people because of where they live:

> *The task here is not to celebrate each and every new possibility qua*
> *possibility, but to re-describe those possibilities that already exist,*
> *but which exist within cultural domains designated as culturally*
> *unintelligible and impossible. If identities were no longer fixed as the*
> *premises of a political syllogism, and politics no longer understood*
> *as a set of practices derived from the alleged interests that belong to*
> *a set of ready-made subjects, a new configuration of politics would*
> *surely emerge from the ruins of the old.*[5]

Ultimately, processes such as these may successfully resignify urban
constituencies deemed lesser or *other,* so deeply engrained in the
built environment, by creating a shared platform where a plurality of
voices constantly and continuously appear to one another. Asserting
this agency through practice – building spaces together, using and
managing spaces together – constructs a more complex, complete city
made whole by acknowledging more of its urban dwellers and their
contributions to urban life.

[5] Butler, J. (1990) *Gender Trouble: Feminism and the Subversion of Identity.* Routledge, p. 203.

T Camp

CHAPTER THREE BY JULIA KING

Why T Camp?

It is in places like T Camp where most of India lives. And the people that live there are the ones who have executed the most change for themselves. They are the only ones who have built enough housing. They are the ones who have tapped into mains when the state has failed to provide. And they often pay the most for electricity and water. And it is important to recognize this. If we as architects/urbanists/designers are concerned about how most of the world lives and the role design can play in addressing issues of social justice and inequality, we must spend time in places like T Camp and learn from those very people who have done the most already and hear the everyday stories of their lives.

Julia King

Stitching the City Together

All images and drawings in this chapter are credited
to Julia King, unless otherwise stated.

pp. 100–101 Overhead view of the T Camp courtyard.

This small courtyard is host to a range of activities from
clothes drying, socialising, playing, to water storage, and
provide multiple access points to second-floor rooms.

Our starting point

This story is part of a body of work that reflects broadly on the ways in which infrastructure design and delivery can influence how citizens make urban space and how we (architects, urbanists, planners, and designers) read the city, with implications for how we intervene.
The past two decades have seen a growing body of literature on infrastructure in urban studies, shifting from a vision of infrastructure as a purely technical endeavour – a "thing", "system" or "output" – to a power-laden process with a physical manifestation.[1] Multidisciplinary approaches have revealed the rich material and social fabric of infrastructure as a dimension of city making,[2] particularly when it operates within AbdouMaliq Simone's provocative notion of "provisioning for the un-provisioned".[3]

It is the story of an attempt to deliver a piece of sanitation infrastructure in a dense urban fabric and of the challenges involved in "designing" something, then seeking to understand why it did not materialise.
The aim of sharing this story is to make visible the rich complexities of urban life and consider methodologies and strategies for intervention by urban practitioners working in the "majority world" context.
The context in question is a small settlement called T Camp, which lies at the heart of central Delhi, one of the world's largest cities, in rapidly urbanising India.

In many ways, T Camp embodies the formally un-provisioned, informally provisioned life characterised by so many settlements eked out in cities around the world. T Camp is a small cluster of informal housing (around 300 households) established over thirty years by a tight-knit network of mostly Bengali inhabitants. The Bengali families live alongside and accommodate an itinerant population of rural-to-urban migrants, who rent rooms carved out of the tight, dense multistorey housing made mostly from brick.

1 Anand, N. (2017). *Hydraulic City: Water and the Infrastructures of Citizenship in Mumbai.* Durham: Duke University Press.; Graham, S. (2010). *Disrupted cities: When infrastructure fails.* New York: Routledge; McFarlane, C., and Silver, J. (2017). "The Poolitical City:

'Seeing sanitation' and making the urban political in Cape Town", in *Antipode*, 49(1), pp. 125-148. McFarlane & Silver (2017)
2 Beall, Jo., Cherenet, Zegeye., Cirolia, Liza., Da Cruz, Nuno., and Parnell, Susan. (2019) "Understanding infrastructure interfaces:

common ground for interdisciplinary urban research?", *in Journal of the British Academy*, 7(s2), pp. 11–43.
3 Simone, A. (2004). "People as infrastructure: Intersecting Fragments in Johannesburg", in *Public Culture*, 16(3): pp. 407-429

Main artery through T Camp.

Walking through the main lane where houses extend
over and above the walkway. Most houses have
some kind of access to the first floor and there are
electricity cables and a range of domestic activities
spilling into the street.

Provisioning sanitation infrastructure

Around 2014, a group of T Camp residents approached a local NGO called CURE (Centre for Urban and Regional Excellence) to help them design and install a municipal sewer to cross the settlement and allow households to connect to the city's formal sewage network. Running through the main arterial route, the pipe, which is only visible from a series of manholes, connected the community to Delhi's sewage network. Years later, I found out that the Pradhan[4] who ran the project had worked as an engineer for Tata[5]. When they relaid the road over the sewer, he decided to dispense with the open grey water drains often used to move rainwater in settlements of this kind, which tend to cause problems ranging from clogging to uncovered flows of effluent. Instead of drains along the side of the path, he designed a series of single covered drains (much like a shower drain), which would drain running water into the sewer. He told me this story when I interviewed him about the project in 2017.

I had been involved in a minor way in 2014 when the sewer was being designed. At the time, I had been asked by CURE to explore how houses with limited space could incorporate a toilet. I had speculatively designed what I called an "infrastructure column", which held a toilet and could be positioned independent of the house above the alley, connecting through the structure to the drain. After some time away from India, I visited T Camp when I returned in 2016 to see the sewer and was intrigued by the way households had and hadn't connected. When the sewer pipe was installed, most households didn't have an in-house toilet to connect to the system, securing their physical connection instead in anticipation of future growth. Households like Dakshina's had connected to the system, with the pipework installed for when they were ready to build their own toilet.

4 The name of a local leader who is often the focal point of contact between government officers and the village community.
5 Tata is an Indian multinational automotive manufacturing company, with headquarters in the city of Mumbai, India, which is part of Tata Group. The company produces passenger cars, trucks, vans, coaches, buses, luxury cars, sports cars, and construction equipment.

Sewer line running through the main lane of
T Camp, only visible from a series of manholes.

Main artery through T Camp.

Concept sketch for the infrastructure column in
T Camp. Drawn before the arrival of the sewage
network, you can see the sketch showing the
municipal drain and considering how a toilet could
connect independent of the house.

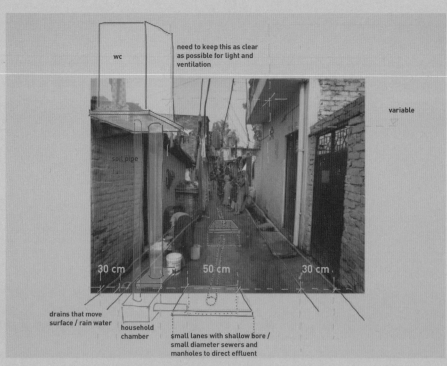

Concept for a structural toilet core.

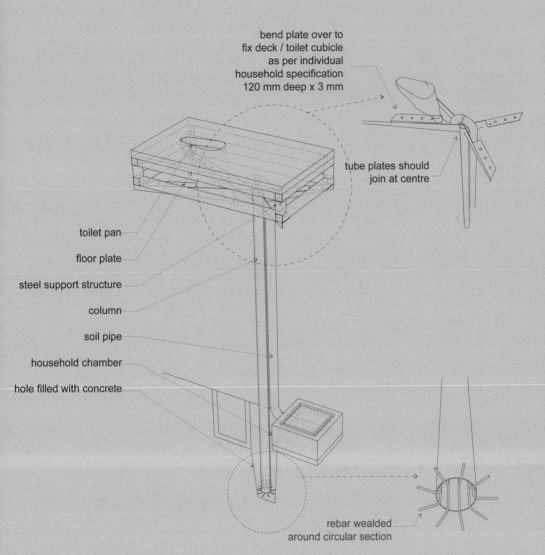

bend plate over to
fix deck / toilet cubicle
as per individual
household specification
120 mm deep x 3 mm

tube plates should
join at centre

toilet pan

floor plate

steel support structure

column

soil pipe

household chamber

hole filled with concrete

rebar wealded
around circular section

Worked-up proposal where the toilet is self-
supporting. Designed to work with local materials
and minimise intervention on the street, the
proposal was to weld rebar to the base of the
circular steel column to stabilise the structure.

I returned in 2017 as I was interested in exploring the relationship between housing investment and sewage infrastructure – a long-standing fascination following my involvement in the design and delivery of a decentralised sewage network in Savda Ghevra, a resettled neighbourhood on the outskirts of Delhi.[6] The idea was to understand the accelerators and barriers to toilet investment two years after the municipal network had been extended. I returned to Dakshina's house to find that her husband had built them a toilet and replaced the former wooden ladder with an integrated concrete staircase-cum-roof. This was an a priori case of "Architecture without Architects". Working with Rashee Mehra, we decided to survey the site to further understand why residents had or hadn't invested in a toilet. Our door-to-door survey asked whether or not the household had a toilet. If it did, questions included: Is there evidence of design thinking? How much did it cost to build? Who built it? If it didn't, the question was: Why not? The act of building a toilet linked homeowners with a network of local actors, including the Pradhan, labourers, masons, material suppliers, financiers, and even brokers. We heard about construction processes that involved no formal plans or contracts but relied instead on networks, trust, and reputation. Local masons would often analyse the house to see how a toilet could be incorporated and then price up the investment, which typically cost 20,000 INR. Where there were no toilets, it was unsurprising to hear many people say that they lacked the funds to build one. What was more surprising was that almost as many people said they hadn't invested in a toilet because of a lack of space. Some households felt their houses could not support additional floors for toilets and/or were too cramped already to install a toilet. With no slack space in the urban fabric, it was impossible to extend beyond the plot.

6 Link: https://www.holcimfoundation.org/projects/decentralized-sanitation-system-near-new-delhi-india

Connection to the sewer ready for when the household has the means to build a toilet.

This image shows the same house the following year once the toilet had been built.

© Nitin Bathla

Toilet	Yes		Toilet	Yes
Floor	First floor		Floor	First floor
Built by	Contractor		Built by	Self-built (husband is a contractor)
When built	Before sewer line		When built	After sewer line
Cost	Over 10,000 INR		Cost	20,000 INR
Reason	Waiting times at public toilet.		Reason	Triggered by sewer construction, and because we have two girls.
Comment	Toilet built before sewer connection and used to connect to another sewer behind T Camp.			

© Nitin Bathla

Toilet	Yes
Floor	Ground floor
Built by	Unknown
When built	After sewer connection
Cost	20,000 INR
Reason	Women didn't like using public toilet at night.
Comment	Toilet on ground floor because no room upstairs. Many families pooled together to by materials for toilet construction (thus reducing cost).

Toilet	Yes (don't use because no door)
Floor	First floor
Built by	Husband (was contractor, now rickshaw driver)
When built	Unknown
Cost	Unknown
Reason	Triggered by arrival of sewer line; and women wanted it because of safety.

111

© Nitin Bathla

Toilet	No, use government toilet	Reason	No space.
Reason	No money, although have space.	Comment	Have laid pipe in anticipation
Comment	House all men, including male		of a toilet.
	renters; so perhaps less of an		
	incentive as there are no women		
	who reside here.		

© Nitin Bathla

Toilet	No
Built by	Has consulted the local contractor regarding costs
Cost	Will cost around 20,000 INR
Reason	The house has been built such that they cannot build another toilet and would have to rebuild the house.
Comment	Have laid a connection pipe in anticipation of a toilet and use this to flush grey (washing, bathing) water.

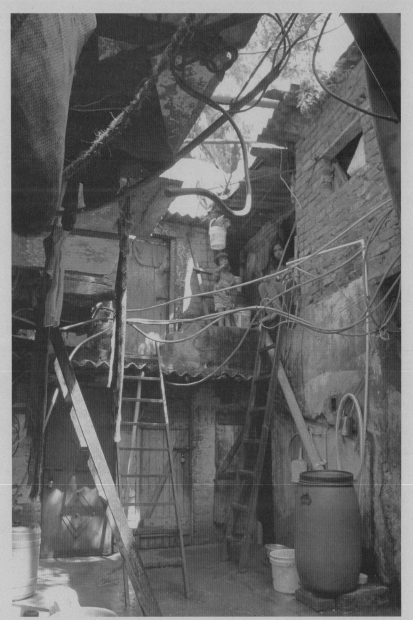

The courtyard and site for the proposed toilet extension.

Visible in this image is the packed courtyard; it is worth noting how access points to the second floor reduce the amount of usable space at ground level.

Designing shared infrastructure

We decided to zoom in on one area to glean further understanding as to why households were not connected despite their access to sanitation infrastructure. Looking at a map by CURE showing all the toilets in T Camp, we could see a courtyard that did not have a single toilet. What we found was an extremely dense collection of ground plus one-storey brick houses. The courtyard itself was a rich collection of ladders, extractor fans, clothes lines, cables, and water butts.

Our starting point was to understand where residents went to the toilet. We focused our attention on the women living in the courtyard through our connection with Sulkeha, an active member of the neighbourhood whose house backs onto the courtyard. Sulkeha took us to the closest public provision – a community toilet complex located a ten-minute walk away in the neighbouring settlement. There, we found a toilet complex with twelve cubicles for women and twenty-two for men, serving a population of approximately 3,500 people. There had been double the number of cubicles for women but half were shut due to women being harassed or subjected to violence – a common problem for public toilets in India.[7] The manager explained that more than 2,000 women used the service from 4 am to 9 am, quite a feat for this piece of public infrastructure. In many ways, the complex demonstrates how public services can be successful if they have stewardship, running water, and security. However, the complex is not open at night, is very busy, and is located at an inconvenient distance. It was at this point that we began to discuss a proposal for a shared toilet in the courtyard to supplement this public provision with the courtyard's residents. Our proposal suggested incorporating a shared circulation space to reduce the ladders into the courtyard and a toilet abutting Sulkeha's back wall.

7 Link: https://wash matters.wateraid.org/blog/ risking-rape-to-reach-a-toilet-in-indias-slums

Map of T Camp showing the toilets.
Most toilets are clustered near the eastern
entrance and along the main road through the
neighbourhood. The grey squares highlight
the courtyards where none of the households
had a toilet despite the sanitation infrastructure
being available. The courtyard where we
focused the intervention is highlighted in this
drawings. © CURE, 2017

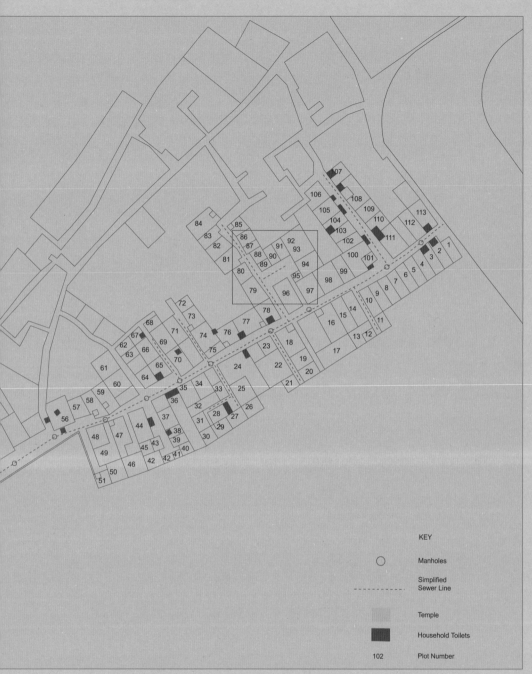

KEY

○   Manholes

- - - - - - -   Simplified
Sewer Line

        Temple

        Household Toilets

102   Plot Number

Design meetings.

Working with the metalsmith.

During the design period, models, drawings and also computer modelling were used to share processes, options, and get feedback.

Consulting with local workmen is central to small-scale city-making processes. In this case we worked with the local metalsmith to design the cheapest demountable structure for the tight space

Local community toilet complex.

The closest toilet for the women of T Camp
who do not have their own, is part of a
community toilet complex serving two (informal)
neighbourhoods. This is the municipal sanitation
infrastructure and "formal' provision for the
3,500+ residents of T Camp and neighbouring
Indra Camp.

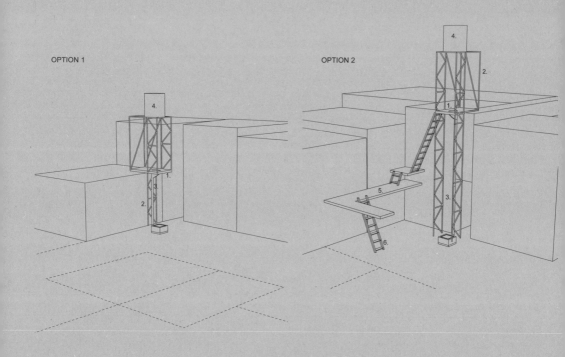

OPTION 1   OPTION 2

PREFERRED OPTION

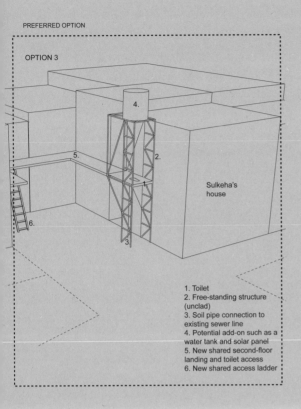

OPTION 3

4.

5.

2.

1.

Sulkeha's
house

3.

6.

1. Toilet
2. Free-standing structure
(unclad)
3. Soil pipe connection to
existing sewer line
4. Potential add-on such as a
water tank and solar panel
5. New shared second-floor
landing and toilet access
6. New shared access ladder

During our consultations with residents,
multiple options for incorporating a toilet into
the courtyard were modelled and represented
in physical models and drawings. This was
critical to driving the discussion forward and
eliciting responses in terms of what was socially,
culturally, and politically possible.

Over the course of this engagement period, we identified three significant barriers: the varying needs of residents, the density (people and architecture), and the gender imbalance. This small courtyard, only slightly larger than a car parking spot, is used by owners and renters, permanent and temporary residents with different priorities. Discussions on investing in the architecture of the courtyard felt out of touch to renters, with some even perceiving that as threatening as they worried their rent would rise if they had better access to toilets. The space was neither neutral nor evenly shared: some families had a greater stake in the space and didn't feel that they should share it equally and relinquish control. There were also tensions as the residents did not all get on, especially two brothers who had no interest in working together. The second issue was finding a location for the toilet that would not obscure light, block access, cause a trip hazard, or create a risk of private encroachment. Some residents worried that those living close to the toilet would take advantage and encroach/build around it to expand their homes. Others worried that the structure would disrupt the hard-fought status quo of the courtyard, which was largely peaceful. Finally, there was a significant gender imbalance among the residents occupying the courtyard. Of the fifty people who lived around the courtyard, only six were women and four were young girls. Inadequate provision of sanitation is felt more acutely by women, who have access to fewer toilets for less time and require more privacy. Yet without a critical mass, the women who occupied the courtyard lacked weight in the discussions.

In order to address these challenges, the final proposal was to trial the project for three months. The residents requested a completely demountable structure and it was agreed that the toilet would only be used at night when the public toilet was shut. After a year of discussions, we felt we had finally achieved our aim. However, a few days later, following a visit to the local market from a state official, a rumour began to circulate that the whole area was to undergo redevelopment. Billboards with 3D visuals of high-rise residential towers and manicured lawns popped up. Suddenly, T Camp faced the threat of eviction and the toilet dropped off the priority list. It was never built.

Learning from failure

In India, more than 6% of the population lack access to safe water and around 15% practise open defecation.[8] The pace of urbanisation – Delhi has witnessed the fastest rate of urbanisation in the world, with a 4.1% rise in population according to the 2011 census – is such that facilities cannot keep up.[9] The idea of universalising services based on centralised models is largely unachievable due to practical considerations, cost, available land, and capabilities. New models and networks are needed. We viewed the toilet proposal as part of an incremental, decentralised extension of sanitation infrastructure by small-scale operators and householders. These kinds of micro-interventions can stitch the city together, producing a thick (albeit precarious) urban fabric of infrastructural access, an example of what sociologist Sylvy Jaglin refers to as "hybrid service delivery configurations".[10] Hybrid delivery systems often rely on co-production to provide and regulate public services through regular, long-term relationships between the state (or any intervening agency) and organised groups of citizens, where both make resource contributions. Hybridity offers solutions that, to quote Gatam Bhan, "recognise the contexts they come from, understand why they have emerged, and then reassess whether the network is the most feasible mode through which to reach the outcomes we want".[11]

8 Link: https://water.org/our-impact/where-we-work/india/
9 Link: https://timesofindia.indiatimes.com/blogs/in-the-name-of-development/cities-of-the-poor-a-view-on-urban-poverty-in-india/
10 Jaglin, S. (2014). "Regulating service delivery in southern cities: rethinking urban heterogeneity", in S. Parnell and S. Oldfield (Eds), *A Routledge Handbook on Cities of the Global South*. London: Routledge. pp. 434–447
11 Bhan, G. (2019) "Notes on a Southern Urban Practice", in *Environment and Urbanization*, 2019; 31(2): pp. 639-654.

In practice, the viability of co-production is considered moot by some, as it requires the state and private sector organisations to recognise and value community-driven approaches and local entrepreneurialism, which is rarely the case. Co-production also relies on utilising sweat equity and poorer citizens to deliver and manage urban services without fully involving or empowering them in this process. This risks institutionalising neoliberal and extractive practices. Although these are legitimate concerns and critiques, if the T Camp project had materialised, it could have delivered a last mile effort to recalibrate decentralised sanitation by extending the community toilet complex at night for women only. The concept represents a model for stitching variegated forms of formal and informal state and market service provisions together. Surveying the agents involved in constructing toilets, many of whom operate on the margins and work in precarious conditions, shows that they cannot be dismissed. They are, in fact, central to the broad project of city-making and work across construction practices in planned and unplanned regimes. With that in mind, stitching together hybrid services is a question of connecting the hard infrastructure, as well as the associated human and material networks.

The critical point of failure was not engagement or long-term maintenance but the urban context in which T Camp exists. These days, urban settings have incredibly dynamic land markets and citizen flows, with infrastructure and people coming and going quickly. This can create a new temporality, which may conflict with the "politics of patience"[12] – the slow, high social investment process required for community-led planning and maintenance. There has been a great deal of scholarship on the legitimising power of water and sanitation,[13] but hybrid, community-led projects take time to design and build. In the face of rapid urban growth, this suggests that the practice of such interventions must be attentive to wider urban configurations and operate at both a macro and micro scale, as well as being resilient to large-scale urban reconfigurations.

With rapid urban expansion, municipalities have struggled to keep pace with the necessary infrastructure, especially due to the peripheral nature of the land available for affordable housing and informal squatter settlements. Development practitioners have long exalted the possibilities of in-situ upgrading, which, in terms of infrastructure, will require these settlements to be stitched to the rest of the city via the extension of existing infrastructure, improvised decentralised systems, and various forms of labour-intensive workarounds. This demands a shift away from the modern ideal of centralised infrastructure provision to more localised, hybrid configurations of diverse (centralised and decentralised) technologies, actors, and organisations. To do this, architects must relinquish control and embrace ideas from multiple experts, such as the Pradhan and his novel drainage solution.

12 Appadurai, A., 2001. "Deep Democracy: Urban governmentality and the horizon of Politics", in *Environment & Urbanization*, 13 (2): pp. 23-43.
13 Anand, N. (2017). *Hydraulic City: Water and the Infrastructures of Citizenship in Mumbai*. Durham: Duke University Press.; Gandy, M. (2011), "Landscape and Infrastructure in the Late - Modern Metropolis", in *The New Blackwell Companion to the City*, pp. 57-65.; Ghertner, A.D. (2011), "The Nuisance of Slums: Environmental Law and the Production of Slum Illegality in India", in Anjaria, J.S and McFarlane, C., (Eds.) (2011), *Urban Navigations Politics, Space and the City in South Asia*. New Delhi: Routledge. Ch.1.

Roof with a toilet.

Small-scale alterations in T Camp
that have happened over time are
visible everywhere you look.

T Camp has not been demolished and the world has since experienced a global pandemic, which has highlighted the need for health facilities in the form of localised "small-loop" solutions working with existing fabrics of place and people. T Camp isn't the failed project – it's the world-class city-making that has failed. When viewed through the lens of Southern urbanism, T Camp offers an infrastructural praxis that allows for a unique kind of hopefulness. Southern urbanism sees emergent cities, and the neighbourhoods that shape them, not as sites to be "fixed" but rather as places of radical experimentation. The kinds of infrastructure that emerge out of Southern practices offer alternatives to the Western networked ideal. A Southern practice asks the practitioner to explore neighbourhoods on their own terms, seeking to understand hybrid, multi-scalar, blurred formal and informal relations, and complex power dynamics.

CRITICAL CONVERSATION

CHAPTER FOUR BY
MATTHEW BARAC
in conversation with
Julia King
Paulo Moreira
Elisa Silva

Why Critical Neighbourhoods?

When discussing a project or a place, we architects will often pick up a pencil and absent-mindedly sketch or draw a diagram on the nearest piece of paper. It helps us think. Although something of a parody of the starchitect genius at work, the well-worn motif of the "napkin sketch" or "back of the envelope" vignette is a reality for many. But for the architects brought into dialogue by this book – Julia King, Paulo Moreira, and Elisa Silva – the creative act neither starts nor stops at the table. They are first and foremost practitioners who do their practising in real places, lived contexts, with others, over a period of time. There is usually a "plan" and there may be many sketches, but both the form and progress of the project are inevitably subject to change.

Matthew Barac

Matthew   This conversation offers an opportunity to go beyond the expository aspects of the work and consider common ground – shared themes and challenges – between the chapter contributions and the neighbourhoods. It may be instructive to move the discussion out of those particular contexts and position it in relation to the three of you: as practitioners on the ground and architects in the studio, as researchers, and as teachers.

Much of the research I do, about cities in the Global South, emerges out of my experience as a professional in architectural practice, but I am now wholly embedded in academic life and so my direction naturally tends towards theory. A recent concern of mine has been to address the question of urban orientation, to ask about how city dwellers find their way, how they feel that they belong, and how they think about their future. It's a topic that can be too easily generalised, but I am talking about cities at the threshold between informality and formality. This interest – in orientation, navigation, and subjectivity – is linked to the theme of personal disposition, and many of the questions that I'm addressing right now are about that. How do you as an urban resident feel yourself to be part of the city? What forms of social and spatial practice constitute cosmopolitan ways of living as an urbanite? How do you establish a claim to belonging while retaining the anonymity, autonomy, and mobility we associate with the freedoms that the modern city is supposed to offer? And in this conversation, what does your stance, capacity, and mode of engagement do to the knowledge and value of your work?

Julia   The focus on disposition is a good place to start. My contribution emerges out of my work in India. In my chapter about T Camp, I'm telling a tale of the architect's endeavour as a practitioner and researcher. The purpose of my story is to learn, to teach myself, as it concerns a failed project. The project did not materialise, but its failure opened up constructive possibilities.

I would like to think about methodology in terms of the interface between research and practice under the umbrella of the overarching context for this discussion which is, of course, development. How do we "make" the city through these participatory practices and processes? And how do we read or see the city? Insight into the reciprocity between making and seeing is something easily taken for granted. A lack of appreciation of the necessary give and take between seeing and making, between understanding and producing the city, is so often the root cause of bad architecture: ideas hurriedly turned into projects before the context has been understood.

My architecturally conceptualised sanitation project at T Camp, a Delhi neighbourhood that many refer to as a slum (a term we all struggle with), followed a pattern of success I had tested elsewhere in India, but things did not go according to plan. My work on the project started as "practitioner", to get the infrastructure plan going. After some time, I adopted the "researcher" persona, aiming to diagnose project uptake and failure dynamics while investigating alternative development options. We progressed the project to the point of negotiating a deal, but then out of nowhere the city announced the slum's demolition to make way for high-value inner city real estate. Despite our work, fostering local decision-making and building social capital along the way, the project was blindsided by unseen, implacable priorities.

Matthew

How does this failed project inform your thinking going forward? Many concerned with the urban context – architects, urbanists, and local residents alike – end up jaded by the litany of disappointments and false starts associated with piecemeal development in neighbourhoods such as T Camp.

Julia

The struggle, in so many cases, is to see what is actually going on – to understand local priorities in relation to an ever-changing picture of what the future may hold. We cannot expect local people who have very little time to know what they want, or what they will do when they don't know what will happen next. I have been thinking about this thicket-like development context in terms of hybridity. I want to ask: what does a hybrid configuration of infrastructure investment look like in neighbourhoods such as this one? Change is now so accelerated and aggressive that the community-driven approaches we learned about in ARCSR,[1] or read about in books by Nabeel Hamdi,[2] which call for an outlook I refer to as a "politics of patience"[3] and which we all naturally champion, are now routinely outrun by events, by transactions happening out of sight, and by the normalisation of uncertainty.

For me, I would say that the politics of patience is no longer tenable. The pace of change means that you don't have the time. If you are going to get things done, you can no longer afford to be patient. Perhaps this calls for a more proactive, pushier form of practice.

Matthew

These reflections on how our mode of engagement might need or want to adapt are useful as we work towards defining the criticality that operates within our practices between architecture and the academy, on the ground and in debate. This is a good moment to turn to Elisa's projects in Venezuela, which should open up our key questions: the question of hybridity that relates to both financial and social commitment, the urban methodology theme raised earlier, and also of course the definition and characterisation of the work itself as neighbourhood places, processes, structures, or interventions.

1 **ARCSR: Architecture of Rapid Change & Scarce Resources:** www.arcsr.org
2 **Hamdi, N. (2004)** *Small Change.* Earthscan.

3 **Appadurai, A. (2001)** "Deep Democracy: Urban Governmentality and the Horizon of Politics", *Environment & Urbanization*, 13(2), pp. 23–43.

Elisa

I appreciate the storytelling approach adopted by Julia. As I write about my work, I find myself expressing the context for practice from the point of view of the "I", from my perspective – a first-person perspective, which, in some ways, is an important reminder of the need to place oneself at the scene.

Our focus in Venezuela is on a different kind of infrastructure: public space. The neighbourhoods I am talking about also suffer from the terminology controversy. We don't say "slums"; we call them "*barrios*". We use this word with some difficulty but after consultating locals we learned that for them it doesn't have a derogatory connotation. The neighbours object more to the term "informal" – they don't like it one bit! Someone might say: "We've been around here a long time! I was born in this neighbourhood," so the idea that an informal area is somehow less viable or "formal" as a place to call home makes no sense.

Matthew

Is there a politics of consolidation to your intentions in that your work might aim to help *barrios* obtain continuity with the city?

Elisa

Venezuelan government lacks the will and perhaps the money to address the critical challenges of neighbourhoods. But we've grown our work, plugging into local municipalities wherever we can. Symbolic gestures on continuity won't change the world (or the city – at least not right away) but the intention is to move the discussion forward. My chapter about La Palomera hopefully brings out the story of how ideas, for example in the form of a manifesto, make an impression at the neighbourhood level and contribute to growing a more expansive understanding of the city.

Matthew

Our dialogue has begun to unpack the question of the paradigm of practice for research and development. Paulo, I would like to turn to you on this in relation to the theme of taking stock of what you have called "critical neighbourhoods" in the form of this book, as a project and as a set of reflections.

Paulo

Since moving from Porto to London fourteen years ago, I have combined teaching and practice and, of course, I also completed my research degree. During this time, my ideals began to diverge from conventional architectural practice. I became fascinated by a wider range of disciplines, places, topics, and methods, and this interest took my doctoral investigation to a neighbourhood called Chicala in central Luanda, the capital of Angola.

My fieldwork centred around survey activity, collecting research data and, more profoundly, mapping a place often absent from official records. This was done in anticipation of Chicala's demolition; we knew it would happen – and then it did, partially, before my very eyes. So, my approach to the situation – all playing out in a kind of urban conflict that was a real-time expression of the latent tension in Luanda – actually opened up other professional opportunities. As the project moved forward, it gained new "lives" beyond my initial intentions. The dismantling of Chicala led me to look at other settlements and camps. I connected with various organisations that promote social change, groups that operate in these hostile conditions. By lending visibility to their practices, including dissident and resistant activities, I was able to better understand the complexities of urban change, all of which contributed to envisaging a more socially inclusive city.

A common thread runs through these activities, and this is becoming clearer to me as we talk. The premise of an inclusive vision of the built environment and the people who inhabit it – it's a kind of mission, a crusade to encourage dialogue between diverse areas of practice and action: architecture, research, politics, education, grassroots groups, social issues. I want to see all these combined into a kind of counter-institutional form of interdisciplinary practice that can showcase projects to demonstrate and diversify these experiences.

Matthew   There is an upbeat spirit to your counter-institutional vision. It reminds us that we are talking about not just ideas and practices, but a kind of disposition that may be a prerequisite for positive practice in this context: a context we may take to represent most of the world rather than the fraction of buildings typically procured as architectural commissions. All three of you are emphasising the value of "thinking like an architect" in neighbourhoods such as Chicala, La Palomera, or indeed T Camp. By this I mean that your way of working always starts with the place itself, ideas about design, all anchored by sensitivity to its occupations and the spatial patterning of belonging.

Paulo   During my research in Chicala, I designed a school in Kapalanga, another neighbourhood on the outskirts of Luanda; this is a built project. Fig. 1–2 My research activity is attached to a large, multi-partner project called Africa Habitat[4] that explores the challenge of sustainable living with a focus on Luanda in Angola and Maputo in Mozambique. Fig. 3–6 A key aim of Africa Habitat is to address forms of socio-urbanistic and housing intervention on the urban margins of contemporary African Lusotopia,[5] with a focus on those that improve the living environment and sustainability of habitat among low-income groups. In light of the wider context of acceleration, as Julia highlighted earlier, the need to understand both the impact of such interventions and how to construct and sustain a more inclusive habitat is becoming increasingly urgent.

4 Africa Habitat is a four-year research project based at the Faculty of Architecture at the University of Lisbon, which is funded by the Fundação para a Ciência e Tecnologia (FCT) and the Aga Khan Development Network (AKDN). Project website: http://africahabitat. gestual.fa.ulisboa.pt/en/

5 The concept of "Lusotopia" was coined by French geographer Louis Marrou in 1992. See Ribeiro, A. B. (2020) *Modernization Dreams, Lusotropical Promises*. Leiden: Brill, p. 5.

Fig. 1–2   Kapalanga School, Viana, Luanda. Project by Paulo Moreira
and Parq Arquitectos. © Kota 50, 2015

The Kapalanga school project emerged from
a prolonged period of community work involving
local teachers, residents, and an NGO (APDES).
The project involved rehabilitating an existing
school and building new classrooms, toilets, and
a perimeter fence. The building was made using
local materials and manual labour, with simple,
cheap building techniques consisting of concrete
frame structures and cement blocks for the walls,
and steel structures and corrugated metal sheets
for the roofs. These solutions proved to be suitable
for local climate conditions, as well as economic
constraints and cultural values. The walls were
finished with a type of plaster made from cement
mixed with reddish earth from the ground. Its
materiality gives the school a textured appearance
and creates a strong link between the various
buildings, the ground, and the surrounding area.

Fig. 3   Gika Waterpoint, Viana, Luanda. Project by Paulo Moreira in collaboration with DW as part of the Africa Habitat research project. © Rui Magalhães, 2022

Fig. 4   Wako Waterpoint, Cacuaco, Luanda. Project by Paulo Moreira in collaboration with DW as part of the Africa Habitat research project. © Rui Magalhães, 2022

Fig. 5   Kilunda Waterpoint, Cacuaco, Luanda. Project by Paulo Moreira in collaboration with DW
as part of the Africa Habitat research project. © Paulo Moreira, 2022

The Luanda waterpoints project improved and adapted three water access points on the outskirts of the city in close collaboration with the local partner in Angola, DW – Development Workshop. The first task was to identify sites for intervention, based on analysis of a photographic survey provided by DW. The next step was to travel to Luanda in April/May 2021 and launch an experimental laboratory around the water access points identified, with participation from local residents and professionals. The process was followed by a second fieldwork trip in October/ November 2021, during which further improvements were made on the ground, prioritising local labour and reused materials.

Fig. 6   Kilunda Waterpoint. © Development Workshop, 2022

Paulo   Related practice work in Portugal that draws on these experiences
includes two design projects in progress on the outskirts of Porto
and Lisbon, which are driven by civic aspirations and have a strong
community focus. Fig. 7-8 More than just design initiatives, these civic
commissions are more complex in form. We managed to gather several organisations, residents' groups, grassroots activists, and NGOs
together and sourced funding for small interventions to improve the
public space, inviting residents to claim it.

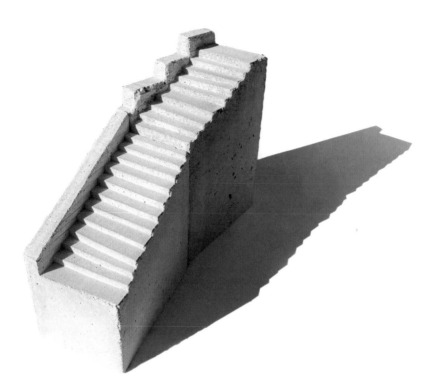

Fig. 7   Model of Monte Xisto connecting stairway, Matosinhos.
Project by Paulo Moreira as part of the Bairros Saudáveis programme.
© Paulo Moreira, 2022

The project in Monte Xisto aims to "stitch up"
an uneven topography characterised by a lack of
connections between the neighbourhood and
the surrounding area. Despite its geographical
proximity to the Leça River valley and the centre
of the parish, the neighbourhood is isolated due
to inadequate access. This physical separation
leads to social exclusion. The aim of the project
was to create new pedestrian routes, improving
access within the neighbourhood and the
surrounding natural and urban landscape.

Fig. 8   Jamaika residents' association, Seixal. Project by Paulo Moreira as part of a partnership with ADSVC and Chão, Bairros Saudáveis programme. © Valter Vinagre, 2022

The project in the Jamaika neighbourhood aims to improve the functioning of a joint facility shared by the local population and neighbouring communities. The starting point for the project was to upgrade an existing building, fitting it with infrastructure and improving its relationship with the outdoors. The project's aims were to stimulate community life in the neighbourhood via activities organised by the residents' association (ADSVC); provide educational activities overseen by Chão – Urban Ethnography Workshop; improve the community's health by opening a medical clinic operating in collaboration with the local hospital; and create an archive open to the public. The centre will serve as a hub for cultural and social development among the community for and with whom it was designed.

Elisa

Learning from what emerges through practice in the Global South and allowing it to inspire practice in the Global North seems more significant than current debates would suggest – I mean articles that target urban scholarship or mainstream architectural media. Clearly, it's not just about the Global South. Perhaps this might be the implication of a counter-institutional architecture practice.

Julia

As a practitioner thinking through the questions and opportunities involved in practising internationally, I have found urbanist Gautam Bhan's insights illuminating. His paper "Notes on a Southern Urban Practice" sets out the limitations of urban scholarship when looking at the Global South if it's not where you come from.[6] He makes a specific, compelling call regarding ownership of the discourse and modes of practice. It's a political provocation opening up to new theoretical formulations.

There is that hybrid of both the practice idiom and practitioner disposition, as well as the knowledge modality in both research and professional terms. Bhan convincingly articulates that Southern question; the issues are very much about colonialism, deep-rooted inequalities, and structural obstacles that exclude people from mainstream city-making.

And he says you *can* ask those questions; you're not limited to Southern cities. His critical outlook puts things in perspective. I found this theorisation as relevant for me when talking about disadvantaged youth in north-west London's Brent as it was when discussing women accessing sanitation in Delhi's informal neighbourhoods. Fig. 9–10 There is something about a Southern practice outlook that is useful in any context of precarity.

6 Bhan, G. (2109) "Notes
on a Southern Urban
Practice", *Environment &
Urbanization*, 31(2):
pp. 639–654.

Fig. 9   © Akil Scafe-Smith 2019

Fig. 10   © Catarina Heeckt 2019

Seen and Heard is a research and engagement project with Brent Youth Parliament and the Blueprint Collective commissioned by Brent London Borough of Culture. During a series of workshops held in summer 2019, twenty-two members of the collective worked with a team of researchers from LSE Cities, led by Julia King, in a summer school environment, where they learned about public space and explored different options for designing it. Over five days of workshops, they built models, went on walkabouts, and met with Quintain, the Wembley Park developers. The outcome of the process was a co-designed space for young people in the new Wembley Park development, a set of policy recommendations for addressing the needs of young people in public space, and the "Yellow Charter", a statement written by the Blueprint Collective calling for young people to be given a greater role in planning and designing public spaces.

143

Paulo   We're all trying to learn from our field experiences in practice and to apply what we have learnt in our home context through teaching, practice, or writing.

Elisa   In Miami, we're working with communities pressured by zoning changes that incentivise investment to redevelop districts predominantly occupied by underprivileged African American residents. Fig. 11 What is happening might be similar to what Julia and Paulo have described in that I am treating our Caracas experience as a precedent for Miami. One learning point is recognising that once we start to understand a place more deeply, certain differences become superficial. Where people are vulnerable and feel they may be displaced, what is the relevant question from our discipline's perspective?

I think that kind of problem – this "research problem" that can be framed as an architectural brief – is transferable from Southern to Northern contexts. Of course, never in generic terms, you always need a wider perspective.

Space for Everyone is a project focusing on six rapidly changing neighbourhoods in Miami, led by Elisa Silva at FIU – Florida International University. The photos show Allapattah, Homestead, Liberty City, Little Haiti, Overtown, and West Grove.

Fig. 11 Space for Everyone. @ Ramses Allende, Tatiana Delgado, Nathaly Guevara, Diana Vazquez (Allapattah); John Correa, Jennyfer Hernandez, Tommy Maldonado, Patricia Perez (Homestead); Tatiana Delgado, Daniel Dussan, Arlinda Haxhiu, Steffania Rivera (Liberty City); Ramses Allende, Fernando Arana, Jose Arroyo, John Correa, Jennyfer Hernandez (Little Haiti); Fernando Arana, Jose Arroyo, Daniel Dussan, Soraya Friedwald, Steffania Rivera (Overtown); Soraya Friedwald, Nathaly Guevara, Tommy Maldonado, Patricia Perez, Diana Vazquez (West Grove)

Julia

I have three things to mention, following on from that. The first concerns the practitioner, whose actions may or may not have consequences. Elisa suggested one might exercise a certain level of tact when writing up practice experiences in the form of research – the question of the "I". When we think about how we work, the "I" should actually be decisively and convincingly acknowledged. John Berger writes: "The way we see things is affected by what we know or what we believe. To look as an active choice. As a result of this, what we see is brought within our reach".[7]

We all agree, as practitioners, that we should avoid reducing complexity, but we need to actively choose to look. I describe my way of doing this is as "unlearning". When I go somewhere new, I try to unlearn my assumptions. I like this idea of engaging with a sort of innocent stupidity, with curiosity and naïveté. A naïve disposition can sidestep the risk of making assumptions. In terms of tools, such as mapping and ethnography, this offers a way to read the situation and find out what's going on. So, in this question of placing yourself at the scene and being open to learning from those around you, it's important to bring the "I" into discussion.

Secondly, and extending the point made earlier about the words we use, a thread here ties into what Paulo's counter-institutional practice implies regarding dissident and resistant actions. I don't identify as an activist, but there's a degree of activism in my projects because they call for reciprocity. They spatialise calls for redressing inequality. In that sense, I am interested in the vocabulary needed in order to speak to power. This concerns the idea of "citizens as collaborators", but even that can be the wrong way to engage in redress because, you know, citizens in neighbourhoods of this kind will always be rendered diminutive by structures of regulation and enforcement. To actually participate does require a different vocabulary to speak to power, because we need to do more than shake the tree.

And thirdly, on the theme of dissemination, I appreciated the framing of sharing your work in progress as a provocation, developing it as a collaborative snowball. Participatory action research as a political project ties us back to the Southern question because that position inherently acknowledges the demand to move beyond materiality. In our projects, we all have to engage with politics.

Matthew

With regard to key themes we have raised – including the vocabularies of engagement, and the politics of visibility and of vision itself – I would be interested to hear your reflections regarding tensions between how the city or neighbourhood is seen and read, on the one hand, and on the other how we change the neighbourhood or change the city.

Julia

I am taken by the point about how the city or neighbourhood appears or may appear to itself. When working on a previous sanitation project in Savda Ghevra where we designed and built a decentralised sanitation system,[8] my theory was that sanitation was the key: that it's what's needed in such settings. I argued that a strategic sanitation intervention can be transformative in the dynamics of incremental urbanism. Fig. 12-18 One can see parallels in theorisations of development by figures like Hernando de Soto, whose approach prioritises tenure.[9] I argued for sanitation (the *de facto* definition of tenure in Indian slums) as the linchpin, and that everything else would come from that.

But then, when you go back to the field and see what has happened over time, you see that things don't always go to plan. The very poor have stayed poor. They were left behind by the dynamics of development because they just didn't have enough money to even start, and this held the neighbourhood back.

In the case of T Camp, as with many inner-city quarters where land values have multiplied, political and commercial adjustments mean that suddenly these slums were getting predatory looks by the city, egged on by the real estate lobby. Despite the benefits of infrastructure initiatives, change still comes aggressively. What transpired in my earlier project, in Savda Ghevra, was an accelerated gentrification at the bottom of the pyramid: low-level developers buying up multiple plots because the addition of infrastructure warrants a mark-up. We saw a sort of developmental bifurcation, thanks to the infrastructure. This undermined aspects of the hypothesis regarding my ethical claims for incremental development.

But looking back through the lens of practice – as Paulo has done – I don't believe my hypothesis was "wrong" as such; it would be very privileged of me to say "development should only happen *on my terms*"! We could all cite examples of projects that failed against expectations, and projects close to one another in zones hungry for development that had opposing outcomes. Understanding how and why these lessons apply genuinely takes time. It entails watching, listening, testing, trying things out. Accepting that fact represents one of the fundamental challenges to practising in sites of informality and poverty: who, if not the academy, will pay for the production of this knowledge?

7 Berger, J. (1972) *Ways of Seeing*. Penguin, p. 8.
8 King, J. (2016) *Incremental Cities: Discovering the Sweet Spot for Making Town-Within-A-City*.

9 De Soto, H. (2000) *The Mystery of Capital: Why Capitalism Triumphs in the West and Fails Everywhere Else*.

Fig. 12–13   Infrastructure network in Savda Ghevra. © CURE, 2013

The infrastructure network in Savda Ghevra
comprised simplified sewers made from narrow
pipes laid at flat gradients under the pavement.
Here, the trenches for these drains and the drains
running through them can be seen cutting through
the narrow alleyways of the neighbourhood.

Fig. 14   Community meeting in Savda Ghevra. © CURE, 2013

Many meetings were held in local parks, where a tent was often put up, and were open to all. Due to the highly gendered nature of the issue of sanitation, women were particularly interested in attending the meetings. In this image, members of the collaborating NGO, CURE (Centre for Urban and Regional Excellence), can be seen talking to a group of women. Community engagement tends to involve numerous meetings and it is a real challenge to make sure that these are not co-opted by certain voices. It is a method where the architect-researcher must be willing to stay for a while, and find and listen to less powerful voices.

Fig. 15   The contract for the sanitation works contained a stipulation that local labour was to be used as much as possible. This image shows a man who lives in Savda Ghevra building one of the many manholes connecting the pipes. © CURE, 2013

Fig. 16   Local built housing in Savda Ghevra, typical to working-class communities in Northern India. © Julia King, 2013

Fig. 17   Community meetings in Savda Ghevra. © Julia King, 2013

In the early stages, before designing the sanitation system, we made a series of cards featuring ten issues, including sanitation, healthcare, and education, which were distributed to attendees to provoke discussion on life in Savda Ghevra. Then a series of chapattis – round discs playing on the image of the bread accompanying each meal – were used to cast votes on the most pressing concern for each individual. The use of chapattis is an original CURE technique employed in many of their projects. Their playful nature enables a more light-hearted approach to important yet often loaded issues.

Fig. 18   Models and coloured straws were used to show how the sanitation project could adapt to different housing types. This process was critical for getting community buy-in for the project. © Julia King, 2013

Matthew   Yes, the familiar medical metaphor applies: for surgery to be effective, you need accurate diagnosis. In these complex informal situations, that depends upon appreciating the reciprocity between practice and research. The argument is that our knowledge about this aspect of urbanism is patchy at best. However, acceptance of the fact of this complexity and the character of the challenge it presents to practice appears to be widening.

We must acknowledge the necessary imperfections and risks of the practice context. Grassroots projects on the ground constitute a messy, multitasking, manifold reality, so any plausible approach to practice must accommodate the conflicts and inefficiencies that will be embedded within its dynamic of productivity. Those who haven't delivered architectural or infrastructure projects on the ground genuinely don't get it! Much of the essential know-how about designing, making, communicating, and implementing comes from practising. Being able to translate it into shareable knowledge is useful, but it does not equate to learning on the job.

Julia   I passionately believe that the architect can have a transformative role in these contexts. Unlike development practitioners, or economists, or lawyers, we can have a concretely real but transformative vision, and we can actually describe what that looks like. So, while I agree that it's a challenging context for practice, it's also a powerful one.

Matthew   The aspect of celebration introduced by Elisa is another vehicle for producing a vision: a mechanism through which the neighbourhood can appear to itself as a community. Where artefacts such as scale models are produced, sometimes with public input or consultation, a focus around which neighbours can come together is provided, grounded in the place they call home. And, when successful, something new is produced: their collectively made and held knowledge.

This transformative process is one in which the knowledge created is diffused into the community of residents, experienced by those involved as a civic moment: knowing who they are entails coming into being as a collective. In some circumstances, it would not be too much to characterise this moment as the neighbourhood's self-actualisation. The community appears to and sees itself, and thus reoriented is better able to understand its position and make decisions about the future. This is, I would suggest, a methodological insight that takes account of the pivotal role the architect can play.

Paulo   My chapter in this book is illustrated by the archive of a photographer who lived in Chicala. He died at the end of 2020, leaving his sons thousands of uncatalogued images. Of course, there is continuity with my earlier work there, but I felt this should be the project now. It's a new addition but another dimension of the Chicala legacy.

Paulo

It occurs to me that, in this commitment we make, the project is never finished. The "early career researcher" will submit a thesis at some point but that is just one stop on the journey, and this book is another stop. In this understanding of practice and its regenerative potential, I imagine a never-ending process. What are we building? The "spatial agency" discourse might call it an "...other way of doing architecture".[10] At some point, I became a collaborator (with the artists, photographer, students, and residents), and as the project evolves it takes on a life that moves into real experiences and spaces. We don't yet know the outcomes. But I feel that in this way of working – a process to find the next step, just going along, not really defining methodological constraints – this is in a way a practice decision. It's like this conversation.

Elisa

My work in La Palomera feels similar; involvement is key but so is collaboration and conversation. As practitioners, we are surely committed to some unlearning – not just as professionals, but unlearning the tropes of how cities operate. It takes an effort to see the city and allow it to appear on its own terms. These development contexts – in Caracas, Delhi, or Luanda – are not laboratories for testing theories but rather environments in which we respond to the invitation to re-examine what we thought we knew.

We've agreed that it brought us a kind of new lens that we're happy now to have in addressing projects anywhere we work – in the North, South, East, or West. This lens reveals a range of insights: about "the politics of patience" as Julia put it, about cycles of time and celebration, and about the challenge of *realpolitik*. I always think of John Turner who said he was "deschooled as an architect" by his eight-year stint in Peru.[11] Turner borrowed from Ivan Illich, who wrote about deschooling as a principle.[12] This is about unlearning the temptation to jump to the answer or solve perceived problems before we have started a wider conversation with stakeholders.

How cities understand themselves is something we can bring to light through processes of unlearning in order to regenerate, as a practice; perhaps a practice led by architects? And there is plenty to learn from the Global South. Cities in the USA typically conceive of themselves in a pattern of submission. There's a service economy model that assumes the municipality should take care of things – but this is like giving away your keys!

10 Awan, N., Schneider, T. & Till, J. (2011) *Spatial Agency: Other Ways of Doing Architecture.* Routledge.

11 Golda-Pongratz, K. (2021) "Reputations: John Turner", in *Architectural Review.* Link: https://www.architectural-review.com/essays/reputations/john-fc-turner-1927
12 Illich, I. (1995) *Deschooling Society.* Marion Boyars.

13 Simone, A.M. (1997) *Urban Processes and Change in Africa.* Coédition NENA/CODESRIA.

Elisa

In La Palomera, we have a community who wants to explore who they are and preserve what they've built. There are lessons about how to actually motivate a community so that it develops resistance to this fragmentation and lack of a civic condition. For the city it's an overwhelming challenge, but at the scale of the neighbourhood people can get a foothold in local continuities if they have somewhere to start. I regularly work with José Carvajal, a journalist and educator, and I find his perspective eye-opening. He talks about "micro-processes" in relation to our intervention efforts. By micro-processes, we mean the things that can instigate a conversation or trigger a meeting; it could be the community organising a festival. The aspiration of self-examination may not be intentional, but in effect that is what is happening: through small-scale engagements, people place themselves in an urban continuity.

Matthew

I am reminded of a foundational text by AbdouMaliq Simone with regard to understanding and depicting African cities in their dynamics of economic, social, and physical reproduction – a metabolic attribute he characterised at the time with the neologism "Africity".[13] Of course, he has subsequently developed this concept, which has proven influential; in his more recent article "People as Infrastructure", he wrote about how informal practices of mutuality and disruption can produce a kind of scaffold. In today's broad effort to reconfigure relations between human and non-human beings – which runs the gamut of overarching metaphors, from "sustainability" to "interdependence" and of course "ecology" – this urban imaginary is a touchstone that allows us to remain faithful to the complexity of life in cities.

Elisa

Cities, when we understand them through micro-processes, are like platforms that can reproduce in ways that are democratic and participatory, that seem hybridised and not explicitly structured but rather organic. This suggests a way of valuing what's there; assets that maybe only a few people know about. Architecturally driven projects will invite prying eyes, so these hidden assets can become visible to people. Needless to say, this makes them vulnerable to being demolished or appropriated for the wrong reasons! But it is an opportunity too. Activities and goods come out into the open and this enhanced visibility through platform processes has benefits.

We talk about diversity as a big plus in a city. The diversity of urban territory in this part of the world, combining *barrios* and *non-barrios*, is essential to the richness of a city. It's a complexity to be celebrated, rather than arguing that a homogenised formal city would be better. Inevitably, you find that a well-intentioned architect will come in with a bad project that has behind it this idea of formalising the context, in a pedantic way. As Julia said, this is the result of not asking the right question.

Matthew
Our conversation and your reflections have articulated these key themes quite productively. Fig. 19 We can gather many of these questions together insofar as they are primarily concerned with reciprocity: about learning from the Global South, about new possibilities for teaching and learning, and about problematising the whole as an orientation towards continuity and the "complete city". As we begin to conclude, I would like to return to the place where this book starts, which is the lifeworld and lived environment of the neighbourhood, and to rehearse this setting in relation to the question of criticality.

The neighbourhood captures, in practical and symbolic terms, this idea of living together, and – for our discussion – where there are precarious circumstances; people feeling insecure, often arriving from somewhere else without friends or connections, as we have learnt from the influential work of Doug Saunders and his formulation "arrival city".[15] Of course, typological categories tend to encourage binary thinking but remain useful as either a provocation or discursive tool. For Saunders, the city of arrival is a "platform", as Elisa described it, for access to the city proper. In the parade of city-themed books seen in the early years of the millennium, Robert Neuwirth's category was "shadow cities", which seems an apposite formulation in relation to the problematic addressed by Julia.[16] Sometimes what the practitioner needs to do is to find out who is lurking in the shadows – to be (as Maurice Mitchell might put it) that "detective".[17]

In these neighbourhoods, what definitions can usefully contribute to expanding the knowledge base so as to address the "majority condition"? We know that the *realpolitik* that holds sway in some such neighbourhoods can be difficult to stomach. Intolerance and treachery are as likely to underpin local protocols as the optimism of festival culture in La Palomera. The lived reality may well embody beliefs and ethical orientations that upend the perhaps liberal sensibilities we assume in one another, and sometimes by default uncritically project across the communities we serve.

There's the question of definitions, as we have begun to rehearse, and there's also the question of practices. Elisa spoke about the potential for practice production of neighbourhood as a social and cultural phenomenon, one in which there is perhaps the opportunity to – one might say – facilitate learning from one another, how to be neighbourly through shared projects, the coproduction of knowledge, and collective celebration. So, what are the practices of neighbourhood making? And should we as architects think of ourselves as facilitators in that way, or do we need our understanding to be attuned to how those practices can stand in the way of making neighbourhoods that really matter to people?

Fig. 19   Clockwise: Paulo Moreira, Matthew Barac, Elisa Silva, and Julia King in conversation, 17 June 2021

15 **Saunders, D. (2011)**
Arrival City: How the
Largest Migration in
History is Reshaping Our
World. **Windmill Books.**
16 **Neuwirth, R. (2006)**
Shadow Cities: A Billion
Squatters, A New Urban
World. **Routledge.**

17 **Mitchell, M. (2012)**
"Architect as Detective,
Narrator and Craftsperson",
 paper delivered at the
Design Tactics and
the Informalized City
Symposium, **CornellAAP,**
Cornell University, USA.

Paulo

The neighbourhood allows us to touch on the scale of architecture while also touching on the urban realm: from the home to the city. It sounds so obvious, but these scales are often kept separate during our professional education. If we start from the neighbourhood, which is a city in miniature, it allows us to look at both the concrete conditions of buildings and also the urban structure holding them together.

I felt this reciprocity between city and dwelling in the particular case of Chicala. If we look superficially at the *musseque* settlement, we don't get the whole story. But if we start to know the rest of the city, we find that there are connections and links: it is a single city. It may be fragmented and mixed up, but it is a continuous city.

Julia

The scale and intermediary functionality is a useful point. In Savda Ghevra, the unit was about 350 households: a neighbourhood unit. I found that to be a useful number to work with. It wasn't so large that you couldn't aspire to achieving some sort of consensus, but it wasn't so small that petty familial disputes would get in the way. It sort of feels like the magic number in my work. One of the key takeaways from my doctoral project was not only an appreciation of the relevance of the unit size, but also that there is this "sweet spot". This is about both people and money: how many and how much. It's the point on the scale where families are not rich enough to be autonomous – they haven't levelled up economically to reach middle-class status, with the result that they don't care – but not so poor that they literally cannot engage because their lives are too desperate and comprise nothing but struggle.

Inherently, the more privileged you are, the less you need to collaborate. Living together is actually such a difficult thing to do. And when you don't have to, when everything is a negotiation, you find that there is a massive weight on the project and a drag on progress, because it's so hard to get anything done or keep going. This observation was one of my "unlearning" lessons, to understand and truly see how these communities are, and to get a sense of how as a practitioner you would have to work with them.

Matthew

The notion of the sweet spot is instructive but so is the point about how privilege fosters disengagement and may become an obstacle to collaboration. I live in a local authority housing estate in Hackney, east London, where many of my neighbours are council tenants; others are "gentrifiers" (like me). We have a Turkish family next door and every now and then the kids will come to the door with a tray on which food will be laid out in bowls covered with cling film, and they'll say: "My mum made too much food, so we've brought you a meal." Of course we return the favour in various ways; it's a kind of exchange of gifts and as with that age-old principle it starts to build solidarity.

This prompts the question of neighbourhood structures of care for one another, which can be quite formalised, especially through events. Exchanges of gifts, or festivals and celebrations where people who would ordinarily be at each other's throats must behave cordially in public, represent neighbourly obligations.

Elisa   The question of how care is expressed and encouraged, and the opportunity to be a good neighbour, resonates with aspects of our activity in La Palomera – specifically the story about giving gifts. My team
enjoyed watching how the exchange of seeds between people, linked
to our gardening intervention, has taken off. This dynamic of gift giving
and exchange, of neighbourliness and care, is present in La Palomera
and there is that sense of solidarity and belonging. Many generations
have always lived in the neighbourhood. That produces a dynamic of
social relations that is enviable.

Reflecting on what we know, and sharing experiences of practice
in conversation, allows us to develop critical distance and awareness
of what we do, and of the field – including where there are gaps that
we should work on. In terms of this ecology of knowledge, I would
say the book *Arrival City* by Doug Saunders was a game changer for
me in understanding the role of these neighbourhoods at the macro-
economic scale. They are neighbourhoods that need to be there. They
are city sectors outside of the capitalist dynamic where people can set
up a starter home and begin to find work, and through the extended
period of arrival and settling down their children eventually get a better education. Upward mobility happens thanks to these neighbourhoods, so they play a critical role for the city and for the country. This
is another way that the descriptor "critical" can be packed into the
definition of a neighbourhood.

Matthew   Aspects of the critical dimension of the neighbourhood have informed
our conversation in several instructive ways, three of which I'd like to
dwell on in a few closing remarks. The first concerns critical practice
in its spatial manifestation. The political implications of making, recording, describing, activating, and situating spaces have come up
in our conversation in both practical and theoretical ways. The "critical" facet owes a debt to Jane Rendell's work at the intersection between art and architecture; in our discussion, the question of politics
inflects the content, context, and modality of practice, and criticality
is therefore comprehensively bound into how we approach engaging
with neighbourhoods.[18]

18 **Rendell, J. (2007)
"Critical Spatial Practice:
Curating, Editing, Writing",
in Rugg, J. & Sedgwick,
M. (eds.)** *Issues in Curating
Contemporary Art and
Performance.* **Bristol:
Intellect Books.**

Matthew

Secondly, the theme of criticality as a condition of endurance and a measure of urgency. We touched several times upon the typicality of situations in our practice and research that endure or deal with marginalised, unjust, and, above all, precarious conditions. Criticality here speaks of the condition of becoming that is also at the edge of extinction: the phrase "situation critical", which we associate with nuclear meltdown or a tipping point where order is overcome by chaos. We are challenged, in our critical project, to "grasp the unknowable" as Edgar Pieterse has put it.[19]

And thirdly, the aspect of our spatial thinking rooted in the discipline of criticism – which, for our purposes, I will relate to architectural criticism. For architects, the genealogy of thinking critically about their practice is anchored by the fundamental role played by criticism not only in learning (by way of the "crit") but also in regard to the interpretive tradition of design criticism. Criticism in this tradition is related to other disciplines, but for architecture the challenge concerns making sense of how a range of factors – practical and symbolic, ethical and aesthetic – come together in space and time.

This final point about criticism has to do with the fundamental principle of articulation we talked about earlier, particularly regarding reciprocity between different levels of engagement in a development situation. The problem of criticality here, therefore, becomes a philosophical problem. What concerns us is the ordering of relations of experience, commitment, and action in a manner that adds up to a sense of the whole. That ordering of elements, which Elisa referred to as "micro-processes" and we have discussed elsewhere as "fragments", is of course architecture's fundamental challenge. It is an ordering that, like the discipline of literary criticism, requires a close reading of the situation so as to ensure an appropriate fit between, as you have all reminded us, what we see and what we make.

19 Pieterse, E. (2011) "Grasping the Unknowable: Coming to Grips with African Urbanisms", *Social Dynamics*, 37 (1): pp. 5-23.

**PERFORMING
THE COUNTER-ARCHIVE**

**AFTERWORD BY
INES WEIZMAN**

The impetus to document the existing environment is more compelling at certain moments in history than others and is often driven by social and political change. The transformation or destruction of buildings, villages, and even cities in contexts of war, natural disaster, or capitalist expansion to make space for new urban developments strengthens the urge to record "what is going to disappear".

Some urban politicians and planners pride themselves with documenting the "before" to celebrate the contrast with the "after". Upon closer examination, the "before" image often takes the form of a low-resolution snapshot, while the "after" image is a professional photograph taken in the apparent comfort of the present.

Since its invention in the mid-nineteenth century, photography has become more than an artistic pursuit concerned with capturing what may soon be an image of the past; it has also served as a political tool used to endorse the city's physical transformation. Politicians, power brokers, and city planners all acknowledge that a new regime can rewrite history by creating or manipulating the "collective" archive. Documentation instruments and methods have primarily been funded and controlled by governmental institutions. These institutions have been particularly eager to harness new techniques and commission photographers to methodically document and record the city *before* it undergoes major change.

This method of taking "before" and "after" images was first used in France, most notably by photographer Charles Marville.[1] Marville was commissioned by urban reformer Baron Haussmann during the reign of Napoleon III to document his large-scale destruction of whole neighbourhoods in Paris. His photographs only appear to capture the "before". In fact, the pictures that Marville took between 1852 and 1878 before the city was transformed were long misinterpreted as nostalgic depictions lamenting the destruction of the "old Paris". However, closer study of the camera angles and perspectives that he used in his pictures, compared with the location of the camera and the

1 Weizman, I. (2015) "Images of Time. Documentary Architecture and the History of 'Before and After' Photography", in Koppelkamm, S. (ed.) *Houses Rooms Voices*. Berlin: Hatje Cantz, pp. 62–73.

picture composition on the maps of the old and new Paris, revealed that Marville used Haussmann's plans for restructuring the city to decide where exactly he wanted to place the camera. The photographer's work complemented Haussmann's plans. The gaze of Marville's camera cut through the fabric almost as ruthlessly as Haussmann's pickaxe teams. The views of the uneven, curving streets with cobblestones, which had already been used for barricades on several occasions, and derelict houses do not paint a nostalgic memory of the premodern city. Rather, they condemn it, for these streets were blocking the way to the modern, hygienic, open city of the future. The impetus of modernism was already present in his views of the old city. It was his vision that transformed the present into the future, long before the city was destroyed and rebuilt anew.

"Before" and "after" images emerged out of the limitations of the early photographic process. The few dozen seconds required to expose a mid-nineteenth century photograph were too long to record moving figures and abrupt events. The result was that people were most often missing from the image; only buildings and other elements of the urban fabric registered. In her 1973 book *On Photography*, Susan Sontag writes about how at the very beginning of photography, in the late 1830s, William H. Fox Talbot noted in a discussion of buildings and monuments that the camera had a special aptitude for recording "the injuries of time".[2] Sontag links photography and death:

> Photography is the inventory of mortality. A touch of the finger now suffices to invest a moment with posthumous irony. (...) Photographs state the innocence, the vulnerability of lives heading toward their own destruction, and this link between photography and death haunts all photographs of people"[3]

To capture an event, two photographs were necessary. The technique was thus useful in representing the consequences of urban conflicts, revolutionary action, and large-scale urban reconstructions. In "before" and "after" photographs, the event – whether natural, man-made, or an entanglement of them both – is missing. Instead, it is captured in the transformation of space. As such, "before" and "after" photographs are the embodiment of a forensic time.[4] They frame a missing event by showing the states that precede and follow it. The missing event has two key implications for those using such photographs to study the results of violence: first, there is an imperative to shift attention from the figure (the individual or action) to the ground (the urban fabric or landscape); and second, these gaps mean that the analysis of any pair must always be supplemented by additional information and interpretation.

Photographs might provide an inventory of mortality, or of what has disappeared, but they also demand the inventory of archive. Every instance of documentation calls for an archive, and every archive asks for an architecture, a system of relations and ordering. The archive is never innocent; rather, it is "critical". It is never merely a repository to store documents, objects, and media. The archive stores the photographs' very materiality, as well as information about the subjects represented. As such, it formalises the informal and reveals the hidden, the ephemeral, the temporary, and the migrant. The fleeting moment is dated, the participants of an event are registered, the author is assigned a right over the image, and the archivist administers the information.

The logic of the archive shares something of the logic of producing and instrumentalising "before" and "after" photography. The production of a "before" image of the city shortly prior to its radical transformation could be seen as a way of "occupying" and "patronising" the immediate past that was designed to legitimise the new regime. The greater the contrast between the situation "before" and "after" the transformation, the more political power these images tend to have. On the other hand, those who produce and collect "before" and "after" images can hold fast-moving developers to account. They become evidence to document a lack of care and compassion, as well as a failure to consider collaboration and consultation with the community. Who holds the document, and how it is governed and performed, matter. Michel Foucault writes:

> The archive is first the law of what can be said, the system that governs the appearance of statements as unique events. But the archive is also that which determines that all these things said do not accumulate endlessly in an amorphous mass, nor are they inscribed in an unbroken linearity, nor do they disappear at the mercy of chance external accidents; but they are grouped together in distinct figures, composed together in accordance with multiple relations, maintained or blurred in accordance with specific regularities; that which determines that they do not withdraw at the same pace in time, but shine, as it were, like stars, some that seem close to us shining brightly from far off, while others that are in fact close to us are already growing pale.[5]

For Foucault, the archive that is never completed or wholly achieved forms the background and horizon for a discursive and performative system that speaks to the past and the present, but also defines what can be said.

The three case studies presented in this book not only build archives, but also perform them in line with the discursive system described by Foucault in his *Archaeology of Knowledge*. To emphasise the community perspective and agency with which the archive and its discourse are constructed, I will describe their work as "performing the counter-archive".

Paulo Moreira's research and collaboration with the community of Chicala on the outskirts of Luanda began in 2010. His collaboration and intervention began with an invitation to design a school. Yet, instead of presenting an initial design proposal as many young architects would do, he refused to work alone.[6] Instead, he moved to Chicala, engaged with the community in a series of collaborations, and partnered for several years with universities in Angola, Portugal, and the UK to work with students who would use similar methods to document that poor, segregated yet fascinating village community inhabiting a particular seafront location in Luanda for several hundred years. Paulo's research and that of his fellow researchers, artists, community members, and activists in Chicala was catalysed by the announcement that the whole neighbourhood was soon to be demolished. This left them little time to document what was about to disappear. I remember how hard we found it to believe that this would really happen. But it did. Between 2013 and 2015, a large part of Chicala was destroyed in the first phase of the so-called Sodimo masterplan, which was intended to "re-develop" the site into a large-scale urban district with high-rise blocks, fast roads, and amenities for wealthier people. The masterplan project was halted halfway through, but the looming threat of imminent destruction impacted on the community's lives and investment in their future in Chicala. Unimpressed by the neoliberal wording from the developers that aimed to tame public resistance in the village community, Paulo developed the Chicala Observatory together with the community, fellow researchers, and friends.

2 Sontag, S. [2005 (1973)] *On Photography*. New York: Rosetta Books LLC, p. 54.
3 Ibid. pp. 54–55.
4 Weizman, E. and Weizman, I. (2014) *Before and After: Documenting the Architecture of Disaster*. Moscow, London: Strelka Press.

5 Foucault, M. (2002) *Archaeology of Knowledge*, Routledge Classics (French: *L'Archéologie du savoir*, 1969), pp. 145–46.
6 Years later, at a different location on the outskirts of Luanda, Paulo Moreira designed and built the Kapalanga School, which is mentioned in the previous chapter.

One of the treasures of this community archive project are the photographs by Kota 50 (aka Paulino Damião), who documented everyday life in Chicala in the mid-1980s in the midst of the civil war. These photographs, along with the recent photographs and mappings produced before Chicala was destroyed, are stored and presented in the Observatory archive. Multiple exhibitions, discussions, and photography workshops arose around them. The conversations and observations preceding the documentation and discussion of the material in the archive formed the backbone of their collaborative work to fight the site's complete erasure and forced resettlement from similarly affected communities along the bay of Luanda.

Elisa Silva's chapter explores several urban sites in La Palomera in Caracas, Venezuela, that had been shut off and surrounded by an expanding city fabric. With a team of architects, planners, and cultural practitioners, Elisa was involved in transforming a former waste collection area and a car park. Again, the role of the architect and designer shifted to encompass designing a support structure for a community-based NGO that would be in charge of its own architecture and cultural life. The NGO would act as a mediator, helping find synergies and cultural and spatial strategies that would consolidate the community's strength and general appreciation. The democratic, transparent work carried out in the community brought about change and bolstered a collective identity. Supporting local knowledge of gardening and carrying out refurbishments contributed to an exemplary upgrade of the sites.

Meanwhile, in the centre of New Delhi, Julia King focuses on a small informal housing site called T Camp. Her collaborative work with the community was intended to provide key infrastructure, such as sanitation. King's design led to an undeniable improvement to the harsh living conditions in this settlement, but it also formalised the settlement's informality. Although these improvements could certainly have paved the way for further

collaborations and community work, the project sadly came to an abrupt end. I can only commend the work of these young practitioners, whose determination, friendship, and care is so courageous and so precious to us all.

The effects of what Serbian architect and theorist Srdjan Jovanović Weiss described in 2005 as "turbo architecture", a kind of global techno culture linked to "greedy dreams of extended individual comfort which result in bunkers of extra-legal wealth, bunkers that we will eventually be tempted to call architecture, places that we will be tempted to call the city"[7], can be observed worldwide. This book situates them on the world map. Although only three case studies are presented, there are many, many more places where enormous urban investments, often designed remotely by foreign planners, displace communities and destroy the continuity of people's lives, knowledge, and memories.

7 Jovanović Weiss, S. (2005) "What was Turbo Architecture?" in *Bauwelt Stadt*, Bertelsmann.